The Essential Social Security Retirement Guide

How to Maximize Your Benefits and Avoid Costly Mistakes

Susan Delaney

Table of Contents

Disclaimer

This book is intended for educational and informational purposes only and does not constitute financial, investment, tax, or legal advice. The information provided is based on general principles and publicly available sources as of the time of writing and may not reflect the most current laws, regulations, or individual circumstances.

Retirement accounts, tax rules, and financial strategies can vary widely based on personal factors such as income, age, employment status, location, and changes in legislation. Before making any financial decisions, including when to claim Social Security, how to coordinate spousal or survivor benefits, or how withdrawals from 401(k) plans, IRAs, or other accounts interact with your benefits, readers should consult with a qualified financial advisor, tax professional, or Social Security specialist who can assess their specific situation.

The author and publisher make no guarantees regarding financial outcomes and disclaim any liability for loss, damage, or adverse results arising directly or indirectly from the use or application of the information contained in this book. Past performance of investments or strategies discussed does not guarantee future results.

By reading this book, you acknowledge and agree that you are solely responsible for your financial decisions and outcomes.

Copyright

For information, contact:
Susan Delaney
publishing@essentialretirementguide.com

eBook ISBN: 979-13-992704-3-3

Paperback ISBN: 979-13-992704-2-6

First published 03/2026.
Printed and bound in the United States.

A Message to the reader

Social Security is one of the biggest financial decisions most people will ever make — and one of the least understood.

A lot of people walk into retirement assuming they'll file when the time feels right. That's an expensive assumption. The timing of your claim, your work history, your marital status, how you've structured your other income — all of it affects how much you actually receive, month after month, for the rest of your life.

File at the wrong time and you could leave tens of thousands of dollars on the table. File at the right time — with a clear strategy behind you — and you can significantly increase your monthly income and protect your spouse long after you're gone.

That's what this book is for.

We'll cover how Social Security is calculated, what "full retirement age" actually means for your benefit, why the timing of your claim is a permanent decision, and how to use spousal and survivor rules to protect your household. You'll also get real examples, practical frameworks, and checklists you can actually use.

You don't need to become a Social Security expert. You just need to understand the rules that matter most — and how they apply to you.

Let's get into it.

Other Books in The Essential Retirement Strategy Series

Practical guides designed to help you make smarter retirement decisions and build long-term financial security.

Available Now

The Essential 401(k) & IRA Retirement Guide

Learn how retirement accounts work, how to maximize contributions, and how to create a smarter withdrawal strategy for long-term financial stability.

The Essential Social Security Retirement Guide

How to maximize your benefits, avoid costly claiming mistakes, and coordinate Social Security with your retirement plan.

The Essential Retirement Tax Strategy Guide

How to reduce taxes on retirement income and build a tax-efficient withdrawal strategy.

The Essential Retirement Income Blueprint

How to turn retirement savings into reliable income streams that last throughout retirement.

Coming Soon

The Essential Medicare Planning Guide

How to select the right Medicare plan for you and protect yourself from unexpected medical expenses.

The Essential Early Retirement Blueprint

Learn how to build a realistic strategy to retire early and learn how to make you money last.

Introduction

Most people don't think hard about Social Security until they're close to needing it. Then it hits them: this is one of the most complicated, most consequential financial decisions they've ever faced, and nobody told them there was a test.

You've probably seen the options — 62, 67, 70 — and wondered what the right answer is. Maybe you've spent time on the SSA website and come away more confused than when you started. Maybe a friend claimed at 62 and regrets it, or a coworker delayed to 70 and swears it was the best move they ever made. The problem is, both of them might be right — for their situations.

That's the thing about Social Security: there's no single "correct" answer.

There's only the answer that's correct for you, given your health, your savings, your spouse, your work history, and your plans. This book walks you through how to figure that out.

We start with how benefits are actually calculated — not the vague overview you find on government websites, but the specific formula that determines your monthly check. From there we cover when to claim, how spousal and survivor benefits work as a household system, how taxes interact with your benefits, what happens if you keep working, and the special cases that trip people up (public pensions, divorce, disability, military service). Along the way you'll find real examples with real numbers, frameworks for making decisions under uncertainty, and checklists for specific situations. By the end, you'll have a clear picture of where you stand and a working plan to move forward.

A Quick Note Before You Begin...

One request: if this guide helps you, leave a short review when you're done. Many people make these decisions with almost no guidance. A sentence about what you found useful can point someone else to a resource they didn't know they needed. Now let's start with the basics.

Chapter 1: Understand the System: Social Security Basics Every Retiree Needs

Chapter at a Glance

What you´ll learn in this chapter:

- Why the fear that blocks most financial decisions is rarely named out loud — and the one question that cuts through it
- How the stories you inherited about money, often before age ten, are quietly steering decisions you think you're making freely
- The difference between scarcity thinking and an honest read of your actual numbers
- Four myths about wealth that keep smart, capable people stuck — and why each one collapses under five minutes of scrutiny
- Why risk tolerance is shaped by lived experience, not fixed personality, and how to recalibrate it deliberately

Estimated reading time: 22 minutes

> FIELD NOTE I once sat with a man who ran a profitable electrical contracting business for over a decade and had never invested a dollar outside his pension. It wasn't a numbers problem. It was a sentence his father used to say at the dinner table thirty years earlier. That's the pattern this chapter is built around — and once you see it, you start seeing it everywhere, including in yourself.

The Fear Nobody Names Out Loud

Ask someone why they haven't invested and you'll rarely get "I'm afraid." You'll get "I haven't gotten around to it" or "I'm waiting for the right time" or "the market seems unstable right now." Every one of those is fear wearing a disguise.

The fear is specific: losing money you worked hard for, and having to explain that loss to yourself, or worse, to someone else. That fear is rational at the extremes — nobody should hand a stranger their life savings — and irrational at the level most people actually operate at, where the real risk isn't the occasional market dip. It's doing nothing for twenty years and calling it safety.

Here's what I tell clients who freeze at this stage: stop trying to eliminate the fear. You won't. Fear doesn't respond to information, and you already know that, because you've read the statistics on compound growth and it hasn't moved you an inch. What moves people is smaller, structured exposure to the thing they're afraid of.

Start with an amount that, if it disappeared tomorrow, would sting but not derail you. For most people starting out, that's somewhere between one and three hundred dollars. Put it into something simple — a broad index fund, nothing exotic — and then do the part everyone skips: watch it. Watch it go down. Watch it come back. Watch a full market cycle if you can stand to wait that long. You're not building wealth with that first three hundred dollars. You're building evidence, in your own nervous system, that a dip is not a catastrophe.

Journaling helps here more than people expect. Not vague journaling — specific. Write the actual sentence your fear says: *I'll lose it all and have nothing to show for the years I worked.* Then write the counter, and make it true, not just positive: *I've lost money before — a bad car repair, a job that fell through — and I rebuilt. I can rebuild from a market dip too.* Affirmations that aren't tethered to something real just feel like lying to yourself, and you'll know it.

Mindfulness gets recommended constantly for money stress, usually vaguely. Here's the specific version that works: before any financial decision over a certain size — pick your number, mine is a thousand dollars — take sixty seconds and ask exactly one question: *Am I deciding this from information, or from a feeling I haven't looked at?* That's it. Not a meditation retreat. Sixty seconds. It's enough to catch the panic sell, the impulse purchase, the decision made at eleven at night after doomscrolling financial news.

The Story You Were Handed

Every culture tells a story about what money means, and almost nobody chooses their story. You inherit it the way that contractor inherited his father's line about a rigged market — absorbed, not examined.

Media doesn't help. Turn on any coverage of wealthy people and you'll get one of two flattened versions: the self-made hero who defied the odds through sheer grit, or the out-of-touch villain who has more than they could possibly need and doesn't deserve it. Both versions are simple enough to fit in a headline, and both are mostly fiction. Real financial lives are slower, messier, and far less cinematic than either story allows — which is exactly why the stories persist. Messy truths don't get clicks.

This matters because those two flattened narratives quietly shape what you think is *possible for you.* If your only mental models for "wealthy" are the ruthless villain and the once-in-a-generation genius, you've unconsciously ruled yourself out. You're neither, so the category doesn't apply to you.

I want to introduce a third category, because it's the one that actually describes most people who build real wealth: the unremarkable and consistent. The dental hygienist who maxed out a retirement account for twenty-eight years and never once made headlines. The couple who bought a modest duplex, lived in one half, rented the other, and quietly paid off two mortgages over fifteen years. Nobody makes a documentary about this. It's not dramatic enough. It's also how most durable wealth actually gets built, and it's a story anyone can step into.

Different cultures carry different relationships to money entirely — some treat it as fundamentally communal, something you build with and share within family and community; others treat it as a private, individual pursuit. Neither is wrong. But if you've inherited a communal money story and you're trying to force yourself into an individualist wealth-building framework you read in a book written for someone else's culture, of course it feels wrong. It is wrong — for you. Part of this work is figuring out which parts of the story you inherited actually fit the life you're building, and which parts you're carrying out of habit alone.

Scarcity Is a Reflex, Not a Fact

Scarcity thinking sounds like realism. That's what makes it dangerous. *I can never get ahead. There's never enough. People like me don't end up wealthy.* Say any of those out loud and they sound like conclusions drawn from evidence. Usually they're not conclusions. They're reflexes, fired long before any actual evidence got weighed.

Here's a test I give clients: next time you catch yourself thinking a scarcity thought, stop and ask — is this a fact, or a feeling wearing a fact's clothing? *I can never get ahead* is a feeling. *I have eleven hundred dollars in savings and a car that needs new brakes* is a fact. The feeling borrows the authority of the fact and passes itself off as equally solid. It isn't.

The shift from scarcity to something more workable isn't about forcing yourself to feel abundant when you don't. That's just another performance, and you'll see through it. It's about catching the reflex and asking one honest question: *is this actually true, or is this the old story talking?*

Reframing setbacks helps too, but not the greeting-card version. When someone loses a job, the instinct is either despair or forced positivity — "everything happens for a reason." Skip both. The useful version is narrower: *this closed a door I didn't choose to close. What door is now open that wasn't open yesterday?* Sometimes the honest answer is "none yet, and that's alright for now." That's still more useful than pretending the loss didn't hurt.

Visualization works, but not as daydreaming. The version that changes behavior is specific and near-term: not "picture yourself wealthy," but "picture the exact conversation you'll have with your partner in six months if you keep the current spending pattern versus if you cut one recurring cost starting this week." Vivid, specific, close enough in time to feel real. Vague future-wealth fantasies don't change Tuesday's decisions. Specific six-month pictures do.

Four Myths That Keep People Stuck

Myth one: income and wealth are the same thing. They're not, and confusing them is one of the most expensive mistakes in personal finance. Income is water flowing through a pipe. Wealth is what you've actually collected in the tank. I've met people earning two hundred thousand dollars a year with less net worth than a teacher earning sixty thousand, because the teacher directed a fifth of every paycheck into assets and the high earner spent up to the edge of the higher number every single month. The number on your pay stub tells you almost nothing about where you'll be in twenty years. What you keep and grow does.

Myth two: you need a lot of money to start investing. This one was mostly true thirty years ago and is almost entirely false now. Fractional shares mean you can own a slice of an expensive stock for the price of a coffee. Low-cost index funds exist with minimums low enough that "I don't have enough to start" stops being a real barrier for most people and starts being an excuse that feels more comfortable than admitting the real barrier is fear or unfamiliarity.

Myth three: budgeting means deprivation. Say the word "budget" and most people picture restriction — no more coffee, no more nights out, a spreadsheet designed to make you feel guilty about existing. That's a starvation-diet mentality applied to money, and it fails for the same reason starvation diets fail: nobody sustains deprivation for long. The alternative is a simple allocation, something like putting roughly half of income toward needs, a bit under a third toward things you actually want, and the rest toward savings and debt. That's not deprivation. That's a plan that still lets you live like a person while quietly building something.

Myth four: generational wealth is only for people who already have money. I understand where this belief comes from — it often feels true, because the visible examples are inherited fortunes. But generational wealth, at its core, is just a decision made early and repeated consistently: to save something, to learn enough to invest it sensibly, and eventually to put a will or a basic estate plan in place so what you've built doesn't get lost to confusion or probate delays. None of that requires starting rich. It requires starting.

Risk Isn't a Number — It's a Fingerprint

Financial advisors love to hand out risk tolerance questionnaires, and the questionnaires aren't wrong exactly, but they miss something. Risk tolerance isn't purely mathematical. It's emotional, and it's personal history wearing a spreadsheet's clothing.

Two people can have identical incomes, identical savings, identical time horizons, and completely different reactions to the same market drop. One panics and sells at the bottom, locking in the loss. The other sees the same drop and thinks *everything's on sale.* The difference usually isn't financial literacy. It's what each of them lived through the first time money got scary.

Look at risk historically and you'll see the same pattern play out at scale. The industrialists of the late nineteenth century who built lasting fortunes weren't the most reckless people in the room — they were the ones who paired bold moves with a clear-eyed sense of what they could actually survive losing. That's the real skill. Not fearlessness. Calibration.

The same pattern shows up in every entrepreneurial story worth telling. The founders who built something lasting weren't gamblers who got lucky once. They took calculated risks, absorbed the ones that didn't pay off, and kept enough in reserve that a bad bet didn't end the whole venture. That's the model worth copying — not the fearlessness, the calibration.

Practically, this means your risk tolerance should shift with your actual life, not stay locked in at whatever number a quiz gave you at twenty-five. Someone a decade from retirement can't afford the same risk profile as someone with forty working years ahead of them, and pretending otherwise because "that's what the questionnaire said three years ago" is how people get caught badly exposed at exactly the wrong moment. Revisit it. Life changes. Your comfort with risk should be allowed to change with it.

Where This Leaves You

None of the barriers in this chapter are unique to you, and none of them are permanent. Fear responds to small, repeated exposure. Inherited stories lose their grip once you actually look at them instead of living inside them unexamined. Scarcity thinking is a reflex you can catch in real time once you know what to listen for. The myths fall apart under five minutes of honest scrutiny. And risk tolerance is something you can recalibrate deliberately, rather than something fixed at birth.

What none of this requires is becoming a different person. It requires becoming a slightly more honest one about what's actually been running the show.

Exercise: Naming Your Barriers

Find twenty minutes and something to write with — paper works better than a phone for this, though a phone will do if that's what you have.

1. Write down one specific financial decision you've avoided in the last year. Not "investing" in general — something specific, like opening a brokerage account or asking for a raise.
2. Underneath it, write the real reason, not the polite one. Not "I haven't gotten around to it" — the actual fear or belief underneath.
3. Trace that belief back one generation. Where did you first hear a version of it — a parent, a grandparent, a specific event? Write the moment down if you can find it.
4. Ask honestly: is this belief still true for your life today, or was it true for someone else's circumstances at a different time?
5. Write one small, specific action — small enough that it feels almost too easy — that would move you past this particular barrier this week.

Come back to what you wrote here as we move through the rest of this book. Most of what follows will give these answers more shape.

Key Takeaways

- Fear about money is rarely named directly; it usually shows up disguised as procrastination or "waiting for the right time." Naming it precisely is the first move that actually works.
- Small, repeated exposure to financial risk builds real confidence. Information alone doesn't; you've had the information for years.
- The stories you carry about wealth were mostly inherited before you were old enough to question them. They can be examined and, where they don't fit your life, set down.
- Scarcity thoughts feel like facts. Test them against actual numbers before you let them make a decision for you.
- Income and wealth are not the same measurement. What you keep and grow matters more than what you earn.
- Risk tolerance is shaped by lived experience, not fixed by personality, and it should be revisited as your circumstances change — not left frozen at whatever a questionnaire said years ago.

Next up: how to actually decide when to claim — the trade-offs between early and delayed filing, how to run a real break-even calculation without needing a finance degree, and what changes once a spouse enters the picture.

Chapter 2: Your Claiming Timeline: When to File for Maximum Impact

Chapter at a Glance

What you'll learn in this chapter:

• The three claiming "lanes" — early, on-time, delayed — and what you actually gain or give up in each one

• How to run a break-even calculation in your head, without a spreadsheet, calculator, or finance degree

• The specific factors that should push your decision one way or the other: health, family longevity, savings, and spousal needs

• How spousal and survivor rules quietly change the math the moment you're married

Estimated reading time: 22 minutes

> ***FIELD NOTE*** *People ask me constantly, "What's the best age to claim?" as if there's a universal answer hiding somewhere in a government pamphlet. There isn't. I've seen the math favor 62 for one client and 70 for another client with nearly identical numbers — because their health, their spouse, and their savings were completely different. This chapter won't give you a magic age. It'll give you the actual process for finding your age.*

For most people, Social Security is the one retirement paycheck that feels genuinely certain. Pensions disappear. Markets wobble. Social Security keeps showing up, adjusted for inflation, as long as you're alive. That certainty is exactly why the decision of when to switch it on carries so much weight.

The government hands you a wide window — anywhere from 62 to 70 — to flip that switch. Inside that window, the system quietly rewards some choices and penalizes others, and those trade-offs ripple through the rest of your financial life in ways that aren't always obvious on day one. This chapter isn't here to push you toward "early" or "late." It's here to help you understand precisely what you gain, what you give up, and how to land on a timing decision that actually fits your life, your spouse, and your broader retirement plan.

Picture your claiming decision as a choice between three levers: claim early, claim around your full retirement age, or delay. Each lever moves your monthly check, shifts the total you're likely to collect over your lifetime, and changes what might eventually be available to a spouse or survivor. In Chapter 1, you saw how your earnings record and the benefit formula set your baseline. Here, we add the missing dimension: time. We'll walk through the key ages, show you how to think about your own personal break-even point, and then layer in the rules that matter most for couples and survivors.

You won't leave this chapter with a rigid rule like "everyone should wait until 70." You'll leave with a process instead: know your FRA cold, weigh early versus delayed benefits honestly, run a simple break-even calculation (even if you hate math — I promise this one doesn't require a spreadsheet), and then fit the result into your health, your income, and your family situation. Along the way, we'll look at real-world examples that mirror the choices you're probably facing right now.

2.1 Early vs. Delayed Claiming: Trade-Offs and Decision Factors

The first step in building your claiming timeline is understanding what "normal" actually means in Social Security terms. That's where full retirement age comes in.

Understanding Full Retirement Age (FRA) and Its Importance

Your full retirement age is the age at which you're entitled to 100% of your primary insurance amount — the benefit you've earned based on your lifetime work record. You can claim earlier or later, but every other timing choice gets measured against this one anchor point.

Under current law, your FRA depends on your birth year. Born in 1960 or later? Your FRA is 67, no exceptions. Born a few years earlier? Your FRA sits somewhere between 66 and 67, in two-month increments. The exact number for you is printed right on your Social Security statement and inside your "my Social Security" account. Looking this up is the very first step of any serious timing decision — don't skip it, and don't guess.

Why does FRA carry so much weight? Because Social Security adjusts your benefit up or down from this age, permanently. Claim before your FRA and you lock in a permanent reduction — your checks stay smaller for the rest of your life. Claim after your FRA and you earn delayed retirement credits, which permanently raise your monthly payment all the way up to age 70. The swing from one extreme to the other can easily run 70–80% in either direction, month to month.

Here's the basic structure, laid out plainly:

• Claim as early as 62: your benefit might be reduced by as much as 30% compared with claiming at FRA, depending on your exact birth year.

• Claim at FRA: you receive 100% of your earned benefit. No reduction, no bonus.

• Delay past FRA, up to age 70: your benefit grows by roughly 8% per year, plus cost-of-living adjustments, for every year you wait. After 70, the growth stops entirely.

These adjustments exist so that, on average, someone who lives to a typical life expectancy ends up receiving roughly the same total lifetime benefit no matter when they start. That's the theory. In practice, almost nobody is exactly "average" — and a lot of people live well past the assumptions baked into the system. That gap between the average and your actual life is where understanding your own circumstances turns timing from a guess into a genuine advantage.

Pros and Cons of Claiming Early

Claiming early — anywhere from 62 up to your FRA — has obvious emotional appeal. After decades of paying into the system, finally seeing money come in feels like closure. For some people it also feels like getting their share before the rules change underneath them. I understand both impulses. But early claiming carries a cost that's easy to underestimate until you see it in writing.

The trade-off, stripped down: you get checks sooner, but every single check is smaller, and that smaller amount follows you for the rest of your life. For someone with an FRA of 67, claiming at 62 means roughly a 30% permanent cut. That doesn't just touch your own income — it can also touch what a surviving spouse eventually receives on your record. (Worth knowing: a spouse's maximum spousal benefit is generally based on your full PIA, not your reduced early-claim benefit — we'll unpack that distinction properly in Chapter 4.)

So when does early claiming actually make sense?

Genuine financial need is the most common, and most legitimate, reason. Laid off at 62, can't find comparable work, savings running thin — waiting until FRA or 70 simply isn't realistic in that situation. Early benefits exist precisely for circumstances like this. They're not a consolation prize; they're the program doing exactly what it was designed to do.

Health is the other major factor, and it's worth being honest with yourself here. If you're dealing with serious health challenges, or your family history points toward a shorter-than-average lifespan, you may reasonably conclude you won't live far into your eighties. In that scenario, smaller checks collected over more years can genuinely add up to more total income than larger checks collected over fewer years. I've watched financial planners walk clients through this math and seen clients choose early claiming anyway — fully understanding the numbers — because it matched their health reality and their personal values. That's not a mistake. That's an informed decision.

But the downsides are real too. A permanently lower benefit means less inflation-protected, guaranteed income as you age — and if you live longer than you currently expect, a choice that felt completely reasonable at 62 can start to feel like a real constraint at 85. If you keep working before your FRA, there's also the earnings test to factor in: earn above a certain threshold and part of your benefit gets temporarily withheld until you reach FRA. (We cover the earnings test in full in Chapter 7 — for now, just know it exists. It doesn't reduce your lifetime benefit, because withheld amounts get credited back later, but it can absolutely create a confusing sense of "missing money" in those early years.)

And finally — early claiming doesn't just affect you. If you're the higher earner in a household and you claim early, that reduced amount becomes the foundation for what a future widow or widower might receive as a survivor benefit. That can leave a surviving spouse with less monthly income at precisely the moment they're most financially and emotionally vulnerable.

So, in short: early claiming makes the most sense when you genuinely need the income now, when health or family history points toward a shorter life expectancy, or when your own benefit plays a relatively small role in your overall plan.

Benefits of Delaying Your Claim

Delaying — particularly past your FRA, up to age 70 — feels counterintuitive to a lot of people. It can feel like turning down money you could be collecting right now. But for many retirees, especially those in decent health with other income sources, this delay is one of the single most powerful financial moves available to them.

For every year you wait past FRA, your benefit grows by roughly 8%, up to 70. That's a guaranteed, inflation-adjusted increase, backed by the federal government, at a time when a genuinely guaranteed 8% return is almost impossible to find anywhere else in your financial life. On top of those delayed credits, your benefit continues collecting annual cost-of-living adjustments the entire time.

Delaying tends to pay off most clearly the longer you live — into your late seventies, eighties, and beyond. Because your monthly amount stays elevated for the rest of your life, every additional year you're alive tilts the total further in favor of having waited. For a lot of retirees — women especially, who statistically live longer on average — the odds of reaching those ages are meaningfully high.

Delaying also functions as a strong inflation hedge. In your sixties and early seventies, you might be perfectly comfortable drawing more heavily from investments or part-time work. As you get older, and perhaps want to take on less market risk or simply have fewer work options available, that larger Social Security check becomes the bedrock your budget can lean on.

For couples, delaying the higher earner's benefit reaches further than just that one person's lifetime income. Because survivor benefits typically key off the deceased spouse's benefit, boosting the higher earner's check through delayed claiming effectively boosts the eventual survivor benefit too. Put another way: waiting can be a way of taking care of whichever spouse ends up living longer.

Delaying isn't right for everyone, and it shouldn't be treated as a default. It assumes you can cover your living expenses from savings, a pension, or work income until that larger check kicks in. It also assumes you're comfortable drawing more from your portfolio earlier in retirement, or working a bit longer than you might otherwise want to. But for people who can genuinely manage those trade-offs, delaying is often one of the most powerful long-term security tools available.

Relatable Scenarios and Mental "Visuals"

Sometimes numbers click better as a story. Picture two friends, Alice and Bob, both entitled to the same full retirement benefit — let's say $2,000 a month at an FRA of 67.

Alice decides to claim as soon as she can, at 62. Her benefit gets reduced by about 30%, landing around $1,400 a month. Bob decides to wait until 70. By delaying three years past his FRA, he earns roughly 24% in delayed credits, pushing his benefit up to about $2,480 a month.

From age 62 to 70, Alice collects eight full years of payments — 96 months at $1,400, totaling $134,400. Bob, meanwhile, gets nothing from Social Security during those same eight years. At 70, his much larger payment finally switches on. From that point forward, he's receiving $1,080 more than Alice, every single month. Over time, that extra $1,080 starts chipping away at the head start Alice built up in her sixties. Picture two lines on a graph: Alice's total benefits climbing early but more gradually, Bob's starting later but rising much more steeply. Eventually those lines cross. Past that crossover point, Bob's total lifetime benefits exceed Alice's — assuming, of course, that both of them are still alive.

That imaginary crossover age is what we'll call the break-even point in the next section. Even before running a single calculation, the broad logic is already visible: early claiming wins if you die relatively young; delayed claiming tends to win the longer you live.

It genuinely helps to sketch a simple timeline on a piece of paper here. Mark 62 on the left, 70 on the right, and your FRA somewhere in the middle, between 66 and 67. Under each age, jot down the approximate monthly benefit from your own Social Security statement. Now imagine shading in the years benefits would be paid under each choice. This rough sketch — and it really can be this rough — makes the trade-off feel a lot more tangible than any single number floating on its own.

2.2 Break-Even Analysis: Simplifying Your Decision

With the basic trade-offs in mind, it helps enormously to have one concrete tool that turns "I think" into "I can see." That's exactly what a break-even analysis does.

What Is a Break-Even Analysis?

A break-even analysis asks one specific question: "If I wait to claim a higher benefit, at what age will the total dollars from those later, larger checks catch up to — and then surpass — what I would have collected by starting earlier with smaller checks?"

It doesn't predict your future, and it doesn't hand you a guaranteed "right" answer. What it does give you is a clear age milestone you can compare against your own expectations about health, longevity, and finances. If the break-even point for delaying from 62 to 70 lands around 80, you can ask yourself directly: "Do I genuinely think I'm likely to live past 80? How does my spouse's situation factor in? Can I actually afford to wait that long?"

That turns a vague worry — "What if I miss out?" — into a concrete, specific conversation about ages and probabilities you can actually reason about. It also keeps you focused on one of the most important truths about Social Security timing: at its core, this is a longevity decision, not a market-timing decision. Tools like break-even analysis don't replace your judgment. They make your judgment a lot better informed.

Step-by-Step Break-Even Calculation (No Actual Math Required)

Here's a simple, mostly "no-math" way to think through break-even, using your own numbers.

First, pull your Social Security statement — paper or online. You'll see estimated monthly benefits for claiming at different ages, typically 62, FRA, and 70.

You can apply this exact same logic to any pair of ages you're actually weighing. Online calculators behind the scenes are doing the same arithmetic with more precision, often layering in assumptions about inflation or investment returns. But even a rough version of this calculation gives you real insight: "If I live beyond my late seventies or early eighties, delaying is likely to pay off in total dollars."

1. Identify the two claiming ages you're seriously weighing. For most people, that's a choice between 62 and 70, or between FRA and 70.

2. Note the monthly benefit at the earlier age and at the later age. For example, your numbers might show $1,400 at 62 and $2,480 at 70.

3. Ask yourself how much more the later benefit pays each month. In this example: $2,480 minus $1,400 equals $1,080. That's your extra monthly income for waiting.

4. Now think about what you'd be giving up by waiting. Delay from 62 to 70 and you forgo eight years — 96 months — of the smaller payment. With these numbers, that's 96 times $1,400, or $134,400 missed.

5. Ask yourself: how long would it take that extra $1,080 a month to make up the $134,400 you missed? Even without precise math, you can ballpark it — a little over 100 months, or roughly 8½ years.

6. Add that 8½ years to your claiming age of 70. That puts your break-even age a little past 78. Live beyond that age and the total

money you'd receive by waiting until 70 starts to exceed what early claiming would have given you.

Factors That Affect Break-Even Points

Break-even analysis doesn't exist in a vacuum. The same set of numbers can look very different once you layer in your health, your work situation, and your family life. The break-even age is a starting point — not a verdict.

Health and family history are the most obvious influence. Robust health at 65, parents who both made it into their nineties — that combination might make a break-even in your late seventies feel like a perfectly reasonable bet on delaying. On the other hand, significant health events, multiple chronic conditions, or a family history of shorter lifespans might make the same break-even age feel unrealistic, tilting you toward earlier claiming instead.

Financial need matters just as much, sometimes more. Maybe the break-even math says "wait," but your actual budget says "I need income now." If claiming early is genuinely the only way to avoid depleting savings too fast, that real-world pressure can outweigh a theoretical lifetime maximum that only pays off decades down the line. Worth asking, though: could small lifestyle adjustments, some part-time work, or drawing a bit more from investments now buy you the option to delay and lock in a larger lifelong benefit instead?

Other income sources — pensions, IRAs, rental income — also shape how you should read your break-even number. If Social Security is just one stream among several, you might feel more comfortable delaying to maximize that guaranteed portion. If Social Security is going to be your primary income source, getting something started earlier may feel more secure, even with smaller checks.

And there's one more, quieter factor: how you feel about risk and flexibility. Delaying is, in a sense, a bet on your own longevity and on the long-term stability of the program's rules. Early claiming is a bet on getting paid sooner and keeping more flexibility with your own savings in the meantime. Neither appetite is objectively correct. There's only what lets you — and, if you're married, your spouse — actually sleep at night.

Using Mental "Visuals" to Simplify

Many people find it useful to picture a simple chart, either sketched on paper or just held in their head: a line of ages running from 62 to 90 along the bottom, and for each claiming age you're considering, a rising line tracking cumulative benefits over time. The early-claiming line starts higher but rises gradually; the later-claiming line starts later but climbs more steeply. Wherever the two lines cross is your break-even age.

You don't need perfect math to see the pattern. Below the break-even point, early claiming wins. Above it, delayed claiming wins. Then layer your own circumstances on top: Do I think I'll land above or below that crossing point? Where does my spouse's likely longevity fall? What other money will I have at different ages along the way?

Treat your own rough sketch as a genuinely useful, hands-on tool — not a placeholder until you "do the real math." Even if you never open a calculator, spending ten minutes drawing your personal timeline can make something abstract suddenly feel specific and clear.

2.3 Timing Considerations for Spousal and Survivor Benefits

Up to this point, we've mostly treated Social Security as an individual decision. For a lot of readers, that's only half the picture. The timing of one spouse's claim can shape the entire household's income — not only while both spouses are alive, but for the spouse who eventually outlives the other. This is exactly where your claiming timeline shifts from a solo choice into a coordinated household strategy.

How Spousal Benefits Depend on When You File

If you're married and one of you earned significantly more over your lifetime, the lower earner may be eligible for a spousal benefit based on the higher earner's record. At full retirement age, the maximum spousal benefit generally runs up to 50% of the higher earner's FRA benefit amount — not the boosted, delayed-credit amount, and not reduced by any early-claiming cuts the higher earner might have taken.

Timing plays a significant role here, and it trips people up regularly. A lower-earning spouse can't receive a spousal benefit until the higher earner has filed for their own benefit. If the higher earner delays, that can also delay when spousal benefits begin — even if the lower earner has already reached, or passed, their own FRA. Conversely, if the higher earner files very early, it can "switch on" spousal benefit availability, but locks those benefits in at a permanently reduced level.

Early claiming by the spouse affects things mainly through the age at which that spouse personally claims. Claim spousal benefits before reaching your own FRA and the spousal amount gets reduced. The higher earner's filing date still matters, because the spouse generally can't receive anything until the higher earner files — but the spouse's maximum spousal benefit is based on the higher earner's PIA, not on whatever reduced retirement benefit the higher earner might be collecting because they claimed early themselves.

This is exactly why couples tend to do much better thinking about their benefits together, rather than as two separate, unrelated decisions. In many cases, having the lower earner claim earlier — even on their own record — while the higher earner waits, strikes a genuinely good balance: near-term income covered, long-term primary and survivor benefit protected.

It's also worth understanding the modern "deemed filing" rules. In most situations today, if you're eligible for both a retirement benefit on your own record and a spousal benefit, applying for one means you're treated as having applied for both simultaneously. You don't get to cherry-pick only the spousal benefit while letting your own quietly grow in the background — except in a narrow set of grandfathered situations. The SSA simply pays you the higher combined amount you're entitled to. Understanding this rule now saves you from planning around an option that, for most people, no longer exists.

Survivor Benefits and Timing

Survivor benefits raise the stakes on the higher earner's claiming decision considerably. When one spouse dies, the surviving spouse is generally entitled to the larger of two amounts: their own benefit, or the deceased spouse's benefit. In other words, widowhood typically means going from two checks down to one — the bigger of the two.

This means the higher earner's benefit amount at the time of death effectively becomes the floor of the survivor's Social Security income. Claim early and lock in a permanently reduced benefit, and that smaller number may be all the surviving spouse has to lean on. Delay and maximize the benefit instead, and the survivor inherits that larger amount — a far more secure foundation for the rest of their life.

A worker's own retirement benefit can keep growing through delayed credits up to 70; survivor benefits themselves don't earn delayed credits in quite the same way. The increase the survivor inherits comes from the higher benefit the worker secured while alive — not from the survivor personally waiting past their own FRA to claim survivor benefits. This is precisely why many planners push higher-earning, healthy spouses to seriously consider delaying: they're not just padding their own check. They're insuring their spouse's future income.

Timing also matters for when survivors first claim. Surviving spouses can often start receiving survivor benefits as early as 60 (or even earlier in special circumstances) at a reduced rate, and later switch to their own benefit if it's grown larger by 70 — or do the reverse. The core idea holds steady throughout: whichever benefit is higher at the time becomes the survivor's check, and the higher earner's earlier timing choices shape that number for decades to come.

Advice for Different Household Situations

Because households vary so much, there's no single spousal or survivor strategy that fits everyone. Still, a few broad patterns tend to hold up.

In couples where one spouse earned significantly more than the other, it often makes sense for the higher earner to delay claiming — sometimes all the way to 70 — to maximize the eventual survivor benefit. The lower earner might claim earlier, either on their own record or as a spouse once eligible, bringing income into the household while that larger check continues to grow.

For couples whose earnings have been more comparable, the calculation shifts. Each spouse's own benefit matters more on its own terms, and both might consider some degree of delay. Coordination still adds value here, but it's a less dramatic effect than focusing everything around one dominant earner's record.

Single retirees — never married, divorced, or widowed — get to simplify the math somewhat. Without a current spouse depending on their benefit, they can focus more squarely on their own break-even age, health, and resources. That said, divorced individuals married at least 10 years may be eligible for benefits on an ex-spouse's record under specific conditions, and widowed or surviving divorced spouses have their own unique survivor options worth exploring — even without a current spouse to coordinate with.

Blended families and households with dependents bring their own wrinkles. Minor children, for instance, may qualify for benefits based on your record once you start collecting, up to certain family maximums. That can tilt the equation toward earlier claiming in some cases, since the value of those child benefits can be substantial — even with your own benefit permanently reduced. In situations like this, timing becomes a question not just about your own lifetime income, but about your children's immediate needs right now.

Practical Decision Steps and Example Scenarios

Pulling all of this together, walk through your decision as a short series of practical questions:

7. What are each spouse's FRA and estimated benefits at 62, FRA, and 70?

8. Who's the higher earner, and who's more likely — based on current health and family history — to live longer?

9. How much income do you need right now, and what other sources can you draw on before claiming?

10. If one spouse died in the next 5, 10, or 20 years, what would the survivor's Social Security income actually look like under different claiming ages?

Consider Mark and Elena. Mark is the higher earner, with an estimated FRA benefit of $2,600 and a benefit of about $3,224 at 70. Elena's FRA benefit is $1,200. They'd like some income by the time Mark turns 67, but they also care deeply about Elena's long-term security.

One approach: Elena claims on her own record at 62, accepting a reduced benefit, while Mark delays all the way to 70. For several years, they live on Elena's check plus withdrawals from savings and some part-time income from Mark. When Mark turns 70, his much larger benefit kicks in — and if he dies first, Elena steps up to that higher amount as his survivor. Their timeline reflects a deliberate trade-off: some financial tightening early on, in exchange for robust, inflation-adjusted income later, including for Elena as a widow.

In a different scenario, suppose Jenna is widowed at 60. She has her own work record and is eligible for survivor benefits on her late husband's record. She might choose a reduced survivor benefit in her early sixties, preserving her own retirement benefit so it can keep growing through delayed credits. At 70, she could switch to her own benefit if it's grown larger. Here, timing isn't simply "early" versus "late" — it's about the sequence in which she taps different benefit types to maximize her lifetime income.

You don't need to draw a complex flowchart to make good choices here, but it genuinely helps to sketch a simple map for your own household: who claims when, what each check might look like, and how that picture shifts if one of you dies earlier or later than expected. Combined with the concepts from earlier in this chapter — FRA, early versus delayed claiming, and your personal break-even age — you now have a clear, practical framework for one of the most consequential timing decisions you'll make in your entire retirement plan.

The Bottom Line

There's no universal "best age" to claim Social Security — there's only the age that's best for your health, your savings, your spouse, and your tolerance for risk. The break-even calculation gives you a concrete number to weigh against your own life expectancy. For couples, the decision stops being two separate choices and becomes one coordinated strategy, with the higher earner's timing carrying outsized weight because of what it means for the eventual survivor.

KEY TAKEAWAYS

• Full retirement age is the anchor for every timing decision. Claim before it and the reduction is permanent; claim after it — up to 70 — and the increase is permanent too.

• Claiming at 62 typically costs you about 30% of your monthly benefit for life. Delaying to 70 typically adds about 24% above your FRA amount.

• Break-even age — usually somewhere in your late 70s to early 80s — is the point past which delaying produces more total lifetime income than claiming early. It's a tool for thinking clearly, not a guaranteed outcome.

• Health, family longevity, financial need, and other income sources all shift where your personal decision should land. There's no single correct appetite for the early-versus-delayed trade-off.

• For married couples, the higher earner's claiming decision shapes not just their own income but the eventual survivor benefit. Many households do best when the lower earner claims earlier for cash flow while the higher earner delays for long-term security.

Next up: how to build your own personal "benefits snapshot" — a one-page summary of exactly where you stand today, so every decision in the rest of this book has real numbers behind it.

Chapter 3: Know Your Numbers: Build a Simple Personal Benefits Snapshot

Chapter at a Glance

What you'll learn in this chapter:

• Why "I think I know roughly what Social Security will pay me" is exactly the gap that causes expensive mistakes

• How to read every meaningful section of your Social Security statement — not just the headline number

• How to estimate future benefits using SSA and third-party calculators without getting lost in formulas

• How to build a one-page personal benefits snapshot you'll actually use for every decision in the rest of this book

Estimated reading time: 23 minutes

> ***FIELD NOTE*** *I ask new clients the same question every time: "What's your estimated benefit at full retirement age?" Most people give me a number with a question mark in their voice. A smaller number still can tell me their actual full retirement age. If that's you, you're not behind — you're completely normal. But normal isn't where you want to be making a permanent, six-figure decision from. This chapter fixes that in about an hour of your time.*

Before you decide when to claim Social Security, you need to know what you're actually working with. Most people carry a vague sense that "Social Security will be there" and an even vaguer idea of how much it might actually pay. Surveys on this are remarkably consistent: a sizable majority of adults say they feel reasonably knowledgeable about Social Security, and yet more than half admit they have no real idea how much of their retirement income it will replace. That gap between confidence and clarity is exactly where bad decisions live — filing too early out of habit, underestimating your real income, ignoring valuable family benefits sitting right there in your statement.

This chapter closes that gap with one practical tool: your own personal benefits snapshot. Think of it as your Social Security dashboard — a single page showing your work credits, the highlights of your earnings record, and your estimated monthly benefit at the ages that matter. It won't contain every technical detail buried in the SSA's systems, and it doesn't need to. Its job is to give you a clear, fast-to-read picture of exactly where you stand, so every later decision in this book has real numbers behind it instead of guesses.

We'll start by walking through your official Social Security Statement — the single most important document for understanding your benefits. You'll see how to access it, what to actually look for, and how to spot the kind of mistakes that quietly cost real money over a 25-year retirement. From there, we'll look at simple ways to estimate future benefits without drowning in formulas or actuarial jargon. You'll see how benefits change depending on whether you claim at 62, FRA, or 70, and how to weigh those numbers against your actual expected spending. Finally, we'll pull everything into a one-page summary you'll keep coming back to as you work through spousal, survivor, tax, and timing strategies in the chapters ahead.

By the time you finish this chapter, you won't have the perfect plan — that comes later, once you've absorbed the rest of the book. But you'll have something more useful for right now: a concrete, personalized snapshot of your own numbers that you can hold in your hand, or pull up on your screen, the moment you need to weigh a decision. In Chapter 4, when we get into spousal and survivor benefits in detail, we'll refer back to this snapshot constantly. For now, let's build it, step by step.

3.1 How to Read and Understand Your Social Security Statement

Your Social Security Statement is the official starting point for serious planning. It's not a generic brochure — it's a personalized report summarizing your earnings history, your work credits, and your estimated benefits for retirement, disability, and survivor protection.

Reviewing it regularly, ideally once a year, is one of the simplest and most valuable financial habits you can build into your life.

Locate Your Statement Online or by Mail

Most people today access their statement online. The Social Security Administration has moved away from automatically mailing paper statements every year, particularly to anyone under 60, in favor of a digital self-service model. This is genuinely good news — your online statement updates regularly and almost always reflects your most recent earnings, rather than a snapshot from whenever the SSA last mailed something out.

To see your statement, you'll need a "my Social Security" account. Setting one up takes a few minutes and involves basic identifying information plus some questions pulled from your credit history. A few of those questions might feel strange — a loan you never took out, an address you don't recognize. In those cases, "this does not apply to me" is usually the correct answer; the system throws in a few wrong options deliberately, as a security check. Once you're through, you can securely view and download your current statement whenever you want.

If you'd rather use paper, or you're simply not comfortable with online accounts, the SSA still mails statements automatically to many people around age 60 and older who don't already receive benefits and haven't set up an online account. If you don't want to wait for that birthday mailing, you can request a statement directly and expect it within a few weeks.

Either way — online or by mail — have your statement open in front of you as you work through the rest of this section. Your benefits snapshot gets built directly from its numbers, so it's worth having it on hand rather than relying on memory.

Identify Your Earnings Record

Once you have the statement, turn to the section listing your earnings history. It's usually on the second page, typically a table showing each year you worked, the amount credited toward Social Security, and the amount credited toward Medicare taxes. This earnings record isn't just a historical recap of your career — it's the raw material the SSA uses to calculate your retirement benefit, full stop.

As you saw in Chapter 1, Social Security benefits are based on your highest 35 years of indexed earnings. The SSA adjusts your past earnings for nationwide wage growth, identifies the 35 highest years (or fewer, if you haven't worked that long), and averages them into your AIME. That number feeds the formula that produces your PIA — the building block for every benefit calculation that follows. If a single year is missing or understated on this table, your calculated benefit may end up lower than it should be. There's no asterisk, no flag, no automatic correction. It just quietly reduces your number unless you catch it.

Reviewing your earnings record isn't optional housekeeping — it's one of the most important checks you can run on your entire financial future. Go year by year and compare the figures against your own tax returns, W-2s, or other records where you can. You don't need to reconcile every single dollar, but you should be actively looking for things like:

• A year when you know you worked, but the earnings are listed as zero.

• A year when the earnings seem dramatically lower than they should be.

• Missing self-employment income that you reported on your tax return.

• Years surrounding a name change or multiple jobs that appear inconsistent.

Errors genuinely happen. Employers misreport wages, or use the wrong Social Security number entirely. Self-employment income gets overlooked if taxes weren't filed quite right. In the gig economy especially — stringing together several part-time or contract roles — it's easy for one of them to fall through the cracks. Left uncorrected, mistakes like these reduce your lifetime benefit, and you'll likely never know unless you go looking.

Find a problem? Don't panic, but don't ignore it either. Contact the SSA and ask what documentation they need to correct the record — usually prior-year tax returns or W-2s. Fixing an error early, while you still have easy access to your old documents, is far simpler than trying to chase down decades-old paperwork right before you retire.

One more detail worth knowing as you review this table: there's a maximum amount of income each year that's subject to Social Security tax and counted toward your benefit — the "contribution and benefit base," sometimes called the taxable maximum. Earnings above that limit don't increase your Social Security benefit, even though they may still be subject to Medicare tax. You don't need to memorize every year's exact limit, but it's genuinely useful to understand that once your income crosses it, the portion above the cap simply doesn't move your benefit at all.

Understand Your Estimated Benefits at Different Ages

For most people, the heart of the statement is the section listing estimated monthly retirement benefits. You'll typically see three numbers: what you'd receive claiming at 62, at your full retirement age, and at 70. These aren't guarantees — they're projections built on your earnings record plus the assumption that you'll keep working at roughly your current income until the stated age. Even so, they're a critical starting point, and far better than a guess.

Full retirement age is the cornerstone here. It's the age at which you can first claim your full, unreduced retirement benefit. Depending on your birth year, your FRA falls somewhere between 66 and 67. Your statement lists it right next to your estimated benefit at that age. This number matters because every adjustment for early or late claiming gets defined relative to it — it's the zero point on the dial.

Claim before your FRA — anywhere from 62 up to the month before you reach it — and your benefit is reduced. The reduction is permanent, calculated monthly: roughly 5/9 of 1% for each of the first 36 months before FRA, and 5/12 of 1% for each additional month beyond that. Work through the math and you land around a 25–30% reduction starting at 62 instead of FRA, depending on your exact birth year. Your statement's age-62 figure already has this reduction baked in.

On the other side, delay past your FRA and your benefit increases through delayed retirement credits — roughly 8% per year, or two-thirds of 1% per month, for every year you postpone between FRA and 70. The age-70 estimate on your statement reflects those credits, and the resulting number is often substantially higher than your FRA figure.

Looking at all three numbers side by side, you're really examining three different retirement scenarios. At 62, you get money sooner but at a lower monthly rate, potentially across more years. At FRA, you get your standard benefit, no adjustment either way. At 70, you wait longer but lock in a higher monthly payment that continues, with cost-of-living adjustments, for the rest of your life. Chapters 2 and 5 will help you decide which path actually fits your life expectancy, health, work plans, and family situation — but for now, your only job is recording these three numbers accurately.

Look for Other Key Information

Beyond the retirement estimates, your statement contains other data that matters enormously for planning, especially for couples and families.

One of the most significant items is your record of work credits. Social Security uses "credits" (sometimes called quarters of coverage) to measure how long you've worked in covered employment. You can earn up to four credits per year, and you generally need 40 — about 10 years of work — to qualify for retirement benefits. The statement shows how many credits you've accumulated, and whether you have enough to qualify for retirement, disability, and survivor benefits.

You'll also see sections summarizing estimated disability and survivor benefits. Disability benefits protect you if a severe medical condition prevents you from working and is expected to last at least a year or result in death. Survivor benefits protect your spouse and dependent children financially if you die. A lot of people skip straight past these sections to get to the retirement numbers, but they're crucial pieces of your household's overall safety net — in Chapter 4, when we get into spousal and survivor strategies, we'll build directly on this information.

Finally, some versions of the statement and related SSA materials include general explanations of spousal and family benefits, plus the conditions under which a spouse or ex-spouse might qualify based on your record. You don't need to master all of those rules right now — just note that the options exist, because they may meaningfully widen the range of strategies available to you later. Your benefits snapshot becomes the bridge between what your statement says today and the claiming decisions we'll work through in upcoming chapters.

3.2 Estimating Future Benefits Without Complex Math

Your Social Security Statement gives you valuable estimates, but it's not the only tool available, and it's built on assumptions that may not match your actual plans. The statement typically assumes you'll keep earning at your most recent income level all the way until retirement age. If you're planning to drop to part-time, retire earlier than that, or expect a significant income jump late in your career, those baked-in assumptions may simply be wrong for you. This is where simple, user-friendly calculators step in — they let you refine the picture without requiring an actuarial degree.

Use the Online Social Security Calculator Tools

The SSA offers several calculators that let you adjust the assumptions behind your benefit estimates. Most people gravitate toward either a quick estimator — enter your birth year and recent earnings, get a fast estimate — or a more detailed tool that lets you input a year-by-year schedule of future earnings. There are also calculators on reputable financial websites that build on your official numbers and provide side-by-side comparisons across different claiming ages.

The real value of these tools is that they handle the complex math for you. You provide the inputs:

• Your date of birth.

• Your current or most recent year of earnings.

• Your planned retirement, or benefit-claiming, age.

• Optionally, a custom schedule of future earnings if you expect a significant change.

The calculator then applies the actual SSA rules — indexing your earnings, computing your AIME, running the benefit formula, adjusting for early or delayed claiming — and produces projected monthly benefit amounts. Some tools let you add a spouse and run spousal or survivor scenarios too, which we'll dig into properly in later chapters.

For now, the goal is straightforward: generate realistic estimates for the same three milestone ages your statement already shows — 62, full retirement age, and 70. If your actual plans differ from the default assumptions, adjust the inputs to match. Planning to stop full-time work at 63 and earn half as much afterward? Enter that into the calculator so your estimate reflects the lower future earnings. It only takes a few minutes, and it makes your one-page snapshot dramatically more accurate.

Focus on Key Milestone Ages for Estimates

In theory, you can claim Social Security in any month between 62 and 70, and the system adjusts your benefit by a fraction of a percent for each month. In practice, almost every planning conversation revolves around the same three anchor ages: 62, your FRA, and 70. Your statement organizes itself around those ages, and you should too.

Age 62 matters because it's the earliest point you can start collecting at all. For a lot of people — especially anyone leaving a physically demanding job, facing a layoff, or dealing with health issues — 62 is genuinely tempting. The trade-off, as covered in Chapter 2, is a permanently lower monthly benefit, typically in the 25–30% reduction range depending on your exact FRA.

Full retirement age, generally 66 to 67, is the neutral point. File then and you get 100% of your primary insurance amount. File earlier and you accept a reduction. File later and you earn delayed credits. Knowing your exact FRA — right there on your statement — is critical, because it defines the "normal" benefit and the schedule of increases and reductions that surround it.

Age 70 marks the end of the line for delayed retirement credits. There's no benefit to waiting past 70 — your benefit simply stops growing. Comparing your age-70 estimate against your FRA and age-62 figures shows you exactly how powerful waiting can be, if your circumstances allow it. For some people, that 8% per year increase between FRA and 70 translates into meaningfully more comfortable and secure income later in life.

Looking at the three estimates side by side tells a simple story: the longer you wait, up to 70, the larger your monthly check. The shorter you wait, the smaller your check, but the sooner it arrives. Later chapters dig into longevity risk, full break-even analysis, and the impact on spouses in much more depth. For now, you're simply gathering the numbers and getting comfortable seeing the trade-offs in concrete terms, on your own statement, with your own dollars.

Avoid Overcomplicating with Formulas

It's easy to get lost in the technical weeds of how benefits are calculated. You'll bump into terms like AIME, PIA, bend points, indexing factors, actuarial adjustments. All of these concepts are real and matter behind the scenes — we covered them properly in Chapter 1 — but you don't need to master the formulas to build a solid benefits snapshot.

Instead, lean on a few simple rules of thumb that translate the math into usable insight:

- Your benefit at full retirement age is your baseline. Think of it as 100%.
- Filing at 62 generally reduces that baseline by roughly 25% to 30%, depending on your FRA.
- Filing after FRA and before 70 increases your benefit by about 8% per year, or two-thirds of 1% per month, in delayed credits.
- Only your highest 35 years of earnings count, and zeros are included if you have fewer than 35 years of covered earnings.

With just these four points, you can make rough estimates without touching a single formula. If your FRA benefit is projected at $2,000 a month, you can quickly approximate that starting at 62 might land somewhere around $1,400 to $1,500 a month, while waiting until 70 could push the benefit above $2,600. The calculators and your statement will sharpen the exact dollar figures, but the conceptual framework is this simple.

This math-light approach works well if numbers genuinely aren't your thing. You can still make a fully informed decision by comparing a handful of key estimates, rather than building out a spreadsheet. And if you happen to be a financial professional reading this, these same rules of thumb let you explain Social Security to clients in plain, relatable terms instead of burying them in formula language.

Compare Your Estimates to Your Financial Needs

Numbers floating on their own aren't especially useful. A $2,000 monthly benefit can feel large or small depending entirely on your cost of living, your other income, and your lifestyle expectations. To make your snapshot genuinely useful, you need to put your Social Security estimates next to your anticipated retirement budget.

Start by sketching a basic monthly retirement spending estimate. Include housing, food, utilities, transportation, health care, insurance, taxes, entertainment, travel, and any regular support you expect to give family members. You don't need a precise budget down to the dollar – a reasonable ballpark is enough at this stage. A lot of people find it easiest to start with their current monthly spending and adjust for the changes they expect in retirement.

Next, line your Social Security estimates for 62, FRA, and 70 up against that spending number. Suppose you expect to need $5,000 a month in retirement and your FRA benefit is estimated at $1,800 – Social Security would cover about 36% of your needs. Claim at 62 and receive $1,350, and you've got a larger gap to fill from other sources. Delay until 70 and your benefit rises to, say, $2,300, and Social Security covers a bit more of your budget – though you also have to fund the years between retirement and 70 from somewhere else entirely.

This comparison accomplishes a few important things at once. It shows clearly that Social Security is meant to be one piece of your retirement income, not the whole puzzle. It highlights exactly how your claiming-age decision interacts with savings, pensions, part-time work, and spending choices. And it helps you – or an advisor you work with – prioritize what to tackle next: Do you need to save more? Work longer? Adjust spending? Coordinate with a spouse's benefits more carefully?

Later chapters walk through those decisions in real detail, including how to blend Social Security with other income, how taxes factor in, and how to protect a spouse if one of you dies first. Right now, your job is simply to build a realistic, honest understanding of how far Social Security will actually go for you. That awareness is what keeps surprises out of your retirement and lets you claim in a way that supports the rest of your plan, instead of quietly undermining it.

3.3 Create a One-Page Summary: Tracking Work Credits & Earnings

You now have the ingredients for a genuinely powerful planning tool: your Social Security Statement, refined estimates from calculators, and an initial sense of how those benefits fit into your retirement budget. The next step is consolidating all of it into a simple, one-page summary you can pull up any time you're weighing a Social Security or broader retirement decision.

Think of this summary as your personal benefits snapshot. It's not an official government document — it's your own customized reference sheet, built in whatever way makes the most sense to you. In Chapter 4 and beyond, we'll keep referring back to this page as we evaluate spousal strategies, survivor protection, and tax planning, so it's genuinely worth a little time getting it right now.

Gather Your Essential Data in One Place

Start by pulling together the key facts from your statement and any updated calculator results. At minimum, your one-page snapshot should include:

• Your full retirement age, as listed on your statement.

• The total number of work credits you've earned, and whether you have the 40 needed for retirement benefits.

• A note on how many years of earnings you currently have, and whether you've reached or exceeded 35 years.

• Your estimated monthly retirement benefits at 62, full retirement age, and 70, from either your statement or your adjusted calculator outputs.

• A brief note on disability and survivor benefits — something like "Qualifies for disability coverage based on current record" or "Survivor benefits available for spouse and minor children," drawn straight from your statement.

If you're comfortable going a little deeper, you can also note your highest-earning years, or simply record that you've already reached the point where zeros are no longer being added to your 35-year history. You don't need to list every individual year — a short line like "35+ years of covered earnings; highest earnings in the last decade" or "Currently 28 years of covered earnings; additional work years will replace zeros" does the job perfectly well.

The point is having everything in one place. That way, you're not hunting through a four-page statement, multiple calculator printouts, and scattered handwritten notes every single time Social Security comes up. Your numbers are visible at a glance, ready whenever you need them.

Use a Clear, Easy-to-Read Layout

Once you know what belongs on the page, think about how to lay it out so your eyes go straight to the most important information. Try breaking the snapshot into a few clearly labeled sections — "Work Credits," "Earnings History," "Benefit Estimates." Inside each section, keep the entries short and focused.

Under "Work Credits," for example, you might write:

• Work credits earned: 44

• Retirement eligibility: Met (40+ credits)

• Disability eligibility: Met (check statement for details)

Under "Earnings History," something like:

• Years with covered earnings: 32

• Highest earnings decade: most recent 10 years on record

• Any zeros in the top 35 years remaining: Yes / No

And under "Benefit Estimates":

• Estimated benefit at 62: $_____ per month

• Estimated benefit at FRA (age ____): $_____ per month

• Estimated benefit at 70: $_____ per month

If you're building this digitally, simple tables or consistent spacing make the information easy to scan. Writing it by hand? Neat, legible headings go a long way. The goal isn't artistic polish – it's quick comprehension. You should be able to pick this page up six months from now and immediately understand your situation, without having to re-read this entire chapter to refresh your memory.

Highlight the numbers you most want to remember. For a lot of people, that's the FRA benefit and the age-70 benefit, since those are the figures most often compared when making timing decisions. Circle them, underline them, color-code them – whatever helps them jump off the page. It's also worth emphasizing your FRA itself, since plenty of rules – like the earnings test, if you claim while still working – are defined relative to that exact age.

Update Your Snapshot Regularly

Your Social Security picture isn't fixed in stone. Every year you continue working and paying Social Security taxes, your earnings record shifts, your top 35 years may improve, and your projected benefit may inch upward. Policy changes, cost-of-living adjustments, and updates to the taxable maximum can all influence your future benefit too. That's exactly why reviewing your statement annually matters so much.

Make it a habit: check your statement once a year, then update your one-page snapshot. Ask yourself:

• Did my total work credits change? (If you haven't reached 40 yet, this matters a lot.)

• Did I add another year of earnings that replaces a lower-earning or zero year in my top 35?

• Did my estimated benefits at 62, FRA, or 70 change noticeably?

• Did the statement note any adjustments in disability or survivor coverage?

Spot any discrepancies in your earnings record during this annual check? Address them right away. Regular review doesn't just catch innocent mistakes — it can also act as an early warning system for identity theft or fraud, if, say, earnings show up under your Social Security number that you don't recognize at all. Your snapshot is your condensed history. Keeping it current is how you stay in control of it.

Consider setting a recurring calendar reminder — "Update Social Security snapshot" — and treating it as part of your yearly financial checkup, right alongside reviewing your investment accounts, insurance coverage, and estate documents. As this book continues, you'll see exactly how to fold that updated information into ongoing decisions about tax planning, Medicare timing, and coordinated claiming strategies with a spouse.

Use Your Summary as a Decision Tool

At this point, your one-page summary has become more than a list of numbers — it's a genuine decision-making tool. Whenever a question comes up — "Should I retire next year?" "Should I delay until 70?" "Can I afford to cut back my hours?" — you can turn straight to this page for context instead of starting from scratch.

Say you're 63 and weighing whether to claim now or wait until your FRA at 67. Your snapshot shows exactly how much more per month you'd receive by waiting, and you can weigh that directly against your savings and other income. You can also see whether continued work will meaningfully add to your record, or whether you've already logged more than 35 strong years — in which case additional work won't move your benefit much, and the decision becomes more about other priorities entirely.

For married couples, this summary becomes especially powerful. In Chapter 4, we'll discuss strategies like having the higher-earning spouse delay until 70 to lock in a larger survivor benefit, while the lower-earning spouse claims earlier. Evaluating that kind of strategy requires comparing each spouse's FRA and estimated benefits at various ages side by side — and having each partner prepare their own one-page snapshot makes that comparison dramatically easier.

Your snapshot also comes into play when we get to taxes later in the book. Social Security benefits can be partially taxable depending on your overall income, and the size of your monthly benefit — combined with withdrawals from retirement accounts, pensions, and other sources — determines how much of it you actually keep after taxes. Being able to quickly reference your projected benefit at different claiming ages helps you model those tax implications far more accurately, and tailor your strategy accordingly.

Most importantly, this simple page builds confidence. Social Security gets described constantly as an overwhelming "big puzzle," and in a sense it is. But distilling your own situation into a clear snapshot means you've put the corner pieces of that puzzle in place. You might not see the whole picture yet — you won't, until you've worked through the rest of this book — but you know its boundaries and its key features. That alone makes every decision that follows noticeably easier.

As you move into the next chapter, keep your one-page summary close. Chapter 4 dives into spousal and survivor benefits and shows you how to layer additional strategy on top of the personal foundation you've just built. Your Social Security numbers — clarified and organized — become the GPS for everything that follows.

The Bottom Line

A vague sense of "Social Security will be around $2,000 a month" isn't a plan — it's a guess dressed up as confidence. The fix takes about an hour: pull your statement, check your earnings record for errors, run a calculator or two with realistic assumptions, and write your own numbers down on a single page. That page becomes the foundation for every other decision in this book, from spousal coordination to tax planning to deciding exactly when to file.

KEY TAKEAWAYS

• Most people overestimate how well they understand their own Social Security numbers. Closing that gap takes about an hour and changes the quality of every decision that follows.

• Your earnings record — the year-by-year table on your statement — is the foundation of your entire benefit. Check it for errors at least once a year; mistakes here permanently lower your benefit if left uncorrected.

• Your three benchmark estimates (62, FRA, 70) on your statement assume you keep earning at your current pace. If your real plans differ, use a calculator to adjust the assumptions and get a more accurate number.

• You don't need to master AIME, PIA, or bend-point formulas to plan well. A few simple rules of thumb — FRA is 100%, 62 is roughly 70–75%, 70 is roughly 124–132% — get you most of the way there.

• Build a one-page personal benefits snapshot covering your FRA, your credits, your three benefit estimates, and a tax note. Update it annually. You'll use this page constantly for the rest of this book.

Next up: how Social Security becomes a household decision the moment you're married — spousal benefits, survivor benefits, and the rules for divorced and remarried couples that most people never learn until it's too late to use them.

Chapter 4: Spousal & Survivor Strategies: Protecting Household Income

Chapter at a Glance

What you'll learn in this chapter:

• How spousal benefits actually work — eligibility, the 50% ceiling, and why claiming early changes everything

• Why the "greater of" rule means some spouses never see a spousal benefit, even when they technically qualify

• What activates survivor benefits, and why the higher earner's claiming age becomes the surviving spouse's income floor for life

• The special rules for divorced and remarried individuals — including the 10-year rule most people have never heard of

Estimated reading time: 24 minutes

> ***FIELD NOTE*** *I've had this exact conversation more times than I can count: a husband says "I'll just claim early, it's fine, we don't need the extra." What he doesn't realize is that he isn't deciding for himself. He's setting the income floor his wife might live on for the next twenty years after he's gone. Once people see it that way, the decision usually changes.*

Retirement planning always feels more complicated once two lives are involved instead of one. You're no longer just asking, "Will I be okay?" You're asking, "Will we be okay — and what happens to whichever of us is left, if something happens to the other?" Social Security's spousal and survivor rules were built to answer those exact questions, at least in part. Yet the rules are genuinely confusing, and a lot of couples either miss out on money they were entitled to, or unintentionally lock in a lower lifetime income without realizing it until much later.

In the last chapter, you focused mainly on your own retirement benefit — how it's calculated, how timing changes the amount, how to think about life expectancy and break-even ages. This chapter zooms out and treats Social Security as a household system. You'll see how your individual benefits interact, how one spouse's decision affects the other, and why the higher earner's claiming age isn't just about their own life — it's about the life of whoever in the marriage lives longest.

We'll walk through three main pillars of household Social Security: spousal benefits while you're both alive, survivor benefits after one spouse passes away, and the special rules for divorced and remarried couples. The same core ideas keep repeating throughout: timing, coordination, protection. Once you understand those themes, the rules stop feeling like a maze and start feeling like a toolkit you can actually use.

As you read, keep two questions in the back of your mind: "What protects our monthly cash flow if one of us stops working?" and "What protects the survivor if one of us dies first?" Your answers will guide not just your Social Security strategy, but your broader planning in later chapters on taxes, investments, and estate design.

Let's start with the benefit most couples hear about first — and understand last: the spousal benefit.

4.1 Understanding and Maximizing Spousal Benefits

Spousal benefits are Social Security's way of recognizing that a lot of households have one higher earner and one spouse who earns less — or didn't earn anything at all under the system. These rules matter especially for couples where one spouse spent years raising children, caring for family members, or working in lower-paying or part-time roles. Think of the spousal benefit as a built-in "income-sharing" feature that can lift your household check even when only one spouse has a strong earnings history.

Eligibility Basics for Spousal Benefits

A spouse is generally eligible for a benefit based on their partner's record once the worker has filed for their own retirement benefit. That spousal benefit can run as high as 50% of the worker's primary insurance amount — the benefit they're entitled to at full retirement age. Notice the phrase "as high as." Claim earlier and that amount shrinks; claim at your own FRA and you can get the full 50%; wait past your own FRA as a spouse and nothing more accrues — there's no delayed-credit growth on the spousal side.

Several basic rules define who actually qualifies.

First, marriage duration. In most cases, you need to have been married at least one full year before you can receive a spousal benefit. This is separate from the survivor and divorced-spouse rules, which we'll get to shortly. Shorter marriages generally don't create spousal eligibility, so couples marrying later in life should keep that one-year clock in mind.

Second, age or children in care. To claim a spousal benefit based on age alone, you generally need to be at least 62. There's a powerful exception, though: if you're caring for a qualifying child of the worker — under 16, or receiving Social Security disability benefits — you can receive spousal benefits at any age, with no reduction for claiming early. This matters enormously for families with disabled children, or for late-in-life parenting situations that don't fit the usual retirement timeline.

Third, the worker has to have filed. As a current spouse, you can't receive a spousal benefit until the higher-earning spouse has actually claimed their own retirement benefit. If your spouse is still delaying their own claim to chase higher retirement credits, your spousal benefit is effectively on hold until they file. (Divorced spouses have an important exception to this rule, which we'll cover in section 4.3.)

Fourth, your own work history doesn't disqualify you. A spousal benefit is available whether or not you've ever worked under Social Security at all. A spouse who never held a job outside the home can still receive meaningful income based purely on the working spouse's record — this is one of the main ways the system protects households built around a single primary paycheck.

These eligibility basics sound simple enough on paper. They get noticeably more nuanced once you bring timing and your own benefit into the picture.

Timing and Coordination Between Spouses

Deciding when each spouse claims is one of the most powerful levers you have for maximizing household income. For couples, the real question is rarely "what's my best age?" in isolation. It's almost always "what combination of ages works best for us as a household?"

There are at least three moving parts for a married couple to track:

1. The higher earner's claiming age.

2. The lower earner's claiming age on their own record.

3. The lower earner's spousal benefit — and when it actually becomes available.

One common pattern: the lower earner claims earlier, sometimes on their own benefit at 62, while the higher earner delays until 67 or even 70. This "split strategy" delivers some near-term income while locking in a larger benefit for the rest of both lives. When the higher earner finally files, the lower earner may step up from their own reduced benefit to a higher spousal amount — subject, of course, to any early-claiming reduction the lower earner already locked in on their own record.

A different pattern emerges when the lower earner has very little or no work history at all. In that case, there's no individual retirement benefit worth claiming early. The couple might instead decide to have the higher earner file at their own full retirement age, so the spouse can receive a full, unreduced 50% benefit — or they might delay the higher earner's claim further if they can comfortably rely on savings for a few more years. Delaying still grows the worker's own retirement benefit and future survivor benefit, even though the spousal portion stays tied to the worker's PIA and never grows beyond it.

Timing here isn't purely about maximizing dollars — it's also about smoothing cash flow and managing risk. Both spouses claiming early might feel comforting right now, but it can permanently reduce whichever spouse eventually becomes the survivor's future income. On the other hand, both spouses delaying might strain savings and raise stress levels in the meantime. The real art is mixing and matching ages so that some income arrives earlier, without sacrificing the long-term security that comes from a larger check later.

This connects directly back to the break-even and life-expectancy thinking from Chapter 2. For a married couple, the relevant horizon isn't just "how long will I live?" — it's "how long will either of us live?" That longer horizon almost always strengthens the case for the higher earner, whose benefit often becomes the survivor's benefit, to delay claiming as long as practically possible.

Impact of Own Benefits on Spousal Benefits

A lot of couples assume the spousal benefit is a completely separate check, added on top of whatever the spouse already earns on their own record. It isn't. Social Security compares two amounts — your individual retirement benefit, and your potential spousal benefit — and pays you the higher of the two. Not both.

Here's how that plays out in practice. Imagine Maria has her own retirement benefit of $900 at her full retirement age, and her husband Joe's PIA is $2,000. Half of Joe's PIA is $1,000. At Maria's FRA, her potential spousal benefit is $1,000. Because $1,000 beats her own $900, she gets effectively "topped up" to $1,000. Social Security frames this internally as her own $900 plus a $100 "spousal excess," but in practice she simply receives one check totaling $1,000.

If Maria's own benefit had instead been $1,200, the comparison flips entirely. Half of Joe's PIA is still $1,000, but Maria's own benefit is already higher. In that case, she'd simply receive her $1,200, with no spousal component at all. Even though she's married to Joe, the spousal rules never come into play, because her own earnings record already provides more than half of his.

This "greater of" rule means a meaningful number of spouses will never receive a spousal benefit, even though they technically qualify for one. It also means early-claiming decisions carry lasting consequences. Claim your own benefit at 62 and you lock in a permanently reduced base amount. When a spousal benefit later becomes available, Social Security doesn't hand you a fresh, full 50% – you receive a combination of your reduced own benefit and a spousal excess, which may itself be smaller depending on when you claimed and when your spouse filed.

Given these overlapping layers, it's genuinely worth comparing side-by-side estimates before making any decision. Online calculators, the benefit estimates inside your My Social Security account, or planning software used by an advisor can all show you how your own and spousal benefits interact at different ages. Even a simple table listing each spouse's expected benefit at 62, FRA, and 70 can clarify whether a spousal benefit is even likely for you, and roughly how much it might add.

Using Restricted Applications and "File and Suspend" Strategies

In earlier years, couples had access to two genuinely powerful techniques: "file and suspend" and restricted applications. Legislative changes have significantly limited both, but you'll still run into them mentioned in older articles and casual conversation, so it's worth understanding what's actually still possible – and for whom.

Historically, a worker could file at full retirement age and then immediately suspend their own benefit. Doing so let a spouse collect a spousal benefit while the worker's own benefit kept earning delayed credits in the background. That "have your cake and eat it too" approach was largely shut down by the Bipartisan Budget Act of 2015. For voluntary suspensions requested on or after April 30, 2016, suspending your benefit also suspends any spousal benefits based on that record, and you can't simultaneously collect spousal benefits on someone else's record while your own is paused.

Deemed filing rules were tightened at the same time. In the past, at full retirement age, you could choose to file only for a spousal benefit and let your own benefit keep growing in the background. Now, if you're eligible for both a retirement and a spousal benefit in the same month you file, you're typically "deemed" to have filed for both, and you simply receive the higher amount. The exception applies to people who turned 62 before January 2, 2016 – they may still be able to use a restricted application at full retirement age to claim only a spousal benefit, letting their own benefit grow untouched.

Here's how a restricted application might work for someone who still qualifies. Suppose Phyllis was 62 by the end of 2015 and has a strong earnings record of her own. Her husband, Charles, claims his own reduced benefit at 62. At Phyllis's full retirement age, because she meets the age cutoff, she can file a restricted application for spousal benefits only. She collects a spousal benefit based on Charles's record while her own benefit continues growing untouched. At 70, she switches over to her maximized retirement benefit — which also becomes the survivor benefit if Charles dies first.

Although these advanced tactics are now limited to a shrinking group of people, they illustrate a concept that still genuinely applies under current law: coordinating your claims so that one benefit acts as a bridge while another grows. Even without a formal restricted application, some survivors can use a similar idea — taking one type of benefit, either survivor or personal, first, and switching later. We'll explore that properly in the next section.

The broader lesson here, as with so much of Social Security planning: rules change. What was standard advice a decade ago might now be impossible, or limited to people born before a specific date. As you build out your long-term plan — which is the entire point of this book — get into the habit of confirming current rules before making any irreversible decision.

4.2 Survivor Benefits: Key Triggers and Optimal Claiming

If spousal benefits are about sharing income while both spouses are alive, survivor benefits are about protecting income once one spouse dies. For a lot of couples — especially those with one significantly higher earner — survivor benefits become the single most important Social Security concept for long-term financial security in the household.

Think back to Chapter 2's emphasis on life expectancy and longevity risk. For a married couple, the real risk isn't just that you might live to 95 — it's that one of you might. Survivor benefits are the mechanism that transfers the higher earner's benefit to whichever spouse lives longer. Planning with that fact in mind can be the difference between a survivor living with genuine dignity and a survivor facing a painful, unexpected drop in income at the worst possible moment.

What Activates Survivor Benefits

Survivor benefits — sometimes called widow or widower benefits — are triggered by the death of a spouse who had enough work credits under Social Security. When that happens, the surviving spouse may be eligible to receive up to 100% of the deceased spouse's benefit, if claimed at their own full retirement age.

To understand what "100%" actually means here, think about the last amount the deceased was receiving, or was entitled to receive — including any reductions from early filing, or increases from delayed retirement credits. That amount, adjusted for cost-of-living increases, becomes the basis for the survivor benefit. In other words, if the higher earner delayed their claim to age 70 and locked in a larger check, that larger amount is what the survivor eventually steps into.

Eligibility comes with a few key conditions. First, you generally need to have been married at least nine months before the worker's death, with exceptions for accidents and certain other circumstances. Second, a surviving spouse can typically claim survivor benefits as early as 60 (or 50 if disabled), though claiming that early comes with a reduction. Third, if the survivor remarries before age 60 (or 50 if disabled), they may lose access to survivor benefits on the prior spouse's record; remarriage after age 60, however, generally preserves that eligibility.

Understanding these triggers before a crisis hits makes an already overwhelming period at least a little less financially chaotic. The right time to learn about survivor benefits is well before you need them — not in the disorienting weeks right after a funeral.

Claiming Survivor Benefits vs. Own Benefits

In a lot of ways, survivor benefits are the most flexible option in the entire Social Security system — if you know how to use that flexibility. A surviving spouse often has a genuine choice between a benefit based on their own work history and a survivor benefit based on the deceased spouse's record. Crucially, survivor benefits aren't subject to deemed filing the way retirement and spousal benefits are. You can claim one type first, and switch to the other later.

That flexibility can be genuinely powerful. A widow in her early 60s, for instance, might claim a reduced survivor benefit at 60 or 62 to restore household income right after her spouse's death, while letting her own retirement benefit keep growing in the background. At 70, she might switch over to her maximized retirement benefit, if it's grown larger than the survivor benefit by then. Or, if her own record is weaker, she might claim her own smaller benefit early and switch to the larger survivor benefit once she reaches her own full retirement age.

Surviving spouses can usually only switch once, and they need to do so before age 70. This makes the timing decision genuinely important. When you're newly widowed, it can feel like the safest move is simply accepting whatever benefit Social Security offers first. But a more deliberate approach — asking "Which benefit should I take first, and when should I switch?" — can meaningfully increase your lifetime income.

One important point worth repeating: deemed filing doesn't apply to retirement and survivor benefits the way it applies to retirement and spousal benefits. The law explicitly treats survivor benefits as a separate category. This means a surviving spouse genuinely has more choice than a married spouse deciding between retirement and spousal benefits while both spouses are alive. It's one of the few corners of the system where the rules are actually more generous than most people assume.

Timing Survivor Benefits for Maximum Impact

As with retirement and spousal benefits, the age at which you claim survivor benefits affects the monthly amount. Claiming as early as 60 reduces the survivor benefit, often significantly. Waiting until your own full retirement age can get you up to 100% of the deceased spouse's benefit. Unlike retirement benefits, survivor benefits generally don't keep increasing past full retirement age purely based on your own age — though the deceased's delayed credits, once earned, still apply.

Timing gets especially nuanced in a few specific scenarios. Consider early widowhood — a surviving spouse in their late 50s or early 60s. In that situation, claiming a reduced survivor benefit at 60 might genuinely be necessary just to keep the household afloat. But that decision also locks in a lower survivor payment, unless the survivor later switches to their own benefit. If the survivor has a strong earnings history of their own, a common strategy is using survivor benefits through their 60s while letting their own benefit grow until 70, then switching over.

Age differences between spouses matter too. If the deceased spouse was significantly older and claimed at 70, the younger survivor might face decades of life relying primarily on that survivor benefit. This makes the original claiming decision of the higher earner even more consequential. In later chapters, when we discuss coordinating Social Security with investments and annuities, this survivor horizon becomes a recurring theme: the goal isn't just protecting the first life — it's protecting the second one too.

Remarriage adds another twist. Remarrying before age 60 can cut off access to survivor benefits based on the prior spouse's record, while remarriage after 60 generally preserves that right. This odd-sounding rule has very real financial consequences, especially for widows and widowers whose first spouse had a much higher benefit. In some cases, couples who are aware of these rules intentionally time their wedding date around them. That may not sound especially romantic, but given that these benefits can run into hundreds of thousands of dollars over a lifetime, it's a perfectly rational thing to consider.

Special Considerations for Disabled or Dependent Spouses

Social Security's survivor framework reaches well beyond older widows and widowers — it also protects families dealing with disability and dependent children. If a surviving spouse is disabled, they can often claim survivor benefits as early as 50. If they're caring for a child under 16, or a disabled child of any age, they may be eligible for survivor benefits regardless of their own age, without the usual reduction for claiming early.

These provisions exist to ensure some level of income keeps flowing into households at exactly the moment they're most vulnerable: right after losing a breadwinner, often while one parent or caregiver is also juggling their own health limitations. Understanding these rules in advance makes it considerably easier to navigate Social Security's application process during what is already an emotionally exhausting time.

In later chapters on risk management and estate planning, we'll come back to the idea of "income layers." Survivor benefits form one of those layers, alongside life insurance, pension survivorship options, and investment withdrawals. The stronger your Social Security survivor base, the less pressure sits on your other assets to provide for a surviving spouse or dependent family members.

4.3 Divorced and Remarried Couples: Special Rules and Opportunities

Up to this point, we've mostly assumed you're married to one person for life. Reality is messier than that. A lot of people marry more than once, divorce later in life, or remarry after losing a spouse. Social Security's rules try to balance fairness to current and former spouses while preventing the "stacking" of multiple benefits at once. The result is a set of divorce and remarriage rules that can be genuinely valuable — but only if you actually know they exist.

Eligibility for Divorced Spouse Benefits

If you're divorced, you may still qualify for spousal benefits based on your ex-spouse's record, as long as certain conditions are met. The most important condition is the "10-year rule": your marriage needs to have lasted at least 10 consecutive years. If it did, and you're now divorced, you can potentially receive a benefit as a divorced spouse once you reach 62 — provided you're currently unmarried, or you meet one of the remarriage exceptions covered below.

A few details surprise people here. First, your ex-spouse doesn't need to have filed for benefits at all in order for you to claim a divorced spousal benefit, as long as both of you are at least 62 and you've been divorced for at least two years. That's a meaningful difference from current spousal benefits, which require the worker to have already filed. Second, your claim doesn't reduce or affect your ex's benefit, or their new spouse's benefit, in any way. Social Security can pay divorced-spouse benefits to multiple ex-spouses from the same worker's record, simultaneously, without any penalty to anyone involved.

The amount works similarly to a regular spousal benefit: up to 50% of your ex-spouse's PIA if claimed at your own full retirement age, reduced if you claim earlier. And just as with current spousal benefits, if your own retirement benefit is higher than the divorced-spouse benefit, you'll simply receive your own instead — you don't get both, Social Security pays whichever is larger.

This is one of the most underused protections in the entire system, almost always because people don't realize they're eligible, or assume claiming on an ex-spouse's record is somehow "taking" something away from that person. It isn't. The system has already fully accounted for this scenario.

Survivor Benefits for Divorced Spouses

Divorced individuals can also qualify for survivor benefits if an ex-spouse dies, as long as the 10-year marriage rule and other standard criteria are met. In that case, the divorced surviving spouse may receive up to 100% of what the deceased ex-spouse was receiving or entitled to receive, subject to the usual reductions for early claiming.

Remarriage rules become especially important here. Remarry before age 60 (or 50 if disabled) and you generally lose eligibility for survivor benefits based on your ex's record. Remarriage after age 60, though, doesn't bar you from divorced survivor benefits at all. This means someone widowed or divorced after a long marriage can preserve survivor rights on that ex-spouse's record, even while entering an entirely new marriage later in life.

As with every survivor situation, divorced survivors get to choose between their own benefit and the survivor benefit. Coordinating those options — deciding which to claim first, and when to switch — can be especially valuable for people whose own careers picked up later in life, after a divorce reshuffled their finances. In these cases, combining a divorced survivor benefit with a growing personal benefit can build a noticeably more secure retirement income path than either option alone.

Impact of Remarriage on Current Benefits

Remarriage doesn't automatically destroy your Social Security eligibility, but it does reshape which record you're able to claim against. For spousal and divorced-spouse benefits, the general rule is straightforward: if you're currently married, you typically claim based on your current spouse's record, not a former spouse's. The moment you remarry, any divorced spousal benefit based on a prior marriage usually ends.

Timing matters considerably here. For survivor benefits, as covered above, remarriage before 60 can block access to survivor benefits on a former spouse's record, while remarriage after 60 preserves them. For regular spousal benefits, once you're remarried, your eligibility shifts to your new spouse's record, following the standard one-year marriage rule for spousal benefits.

These rules create some genuinely interesting planning questions for people entering second or third marriages later in life. Suppose you're 59, divorced after a 20-year marriage to a higher earner, and thinking about remarrying. Marry at 59 and you could lose eligibility for divorced spousal and potential survivor benefits on your ex's record. Wait until you're 60, though, and you may preserve survivor eligibility even after remarrying. Some couples, fully aware of these rules, deliberately time their wedding date around them. That might sound like an unromantic way to think about marriage — but given that these benefits can amount to hundreds of thousands of dollars over a lifetime, it's a perfectly rational consideration to factor in.

Strategies to Maximize Benefits Across Multiple Marriages

When multiple marriages each meet the 10-year rule, you might be eligible for benefits based on more than one ex-spouse's record. You still can't collect more than one benefit at a time, but you may have a genuine choice of the highest amount at each stage of your life. Social Security won't automatically scan every ex-spouse you've ever had to figure out which record works best for you. That's entirely on you — know your own history, and ask.

Consider someone married to Spouse A for 15 years, divorced, then married to Spouse B for 12 years before divorcing again, and now single. At retirement, that person may be able to claim divorced spousal benefits based on whichever ex has the higher PIA, as long as all the eligibility rules are met. If Spouse A later passes away, that same person might claim divorced survivor benefits based on Spouse A's record instead — again choosing between their own benefit and that survivor benefit for whichever produces the better outcome.

In some cases, it makes sense to claim divorced spousal benefits early — as soon as 62 — while letting your own retirement benefit grow until 70. This mirrors the "spousal as a bridge" planning concept some married couples used in earlier years. Once your own benefit surpasses the divorced spousal benefit, you switch over and lock in the higher amount for life.

The common thread running through all of these complicated situations: Social Security, despite its rigid-feeling rules, offers considerable flexibility once you actually understand your options. For married, widowed, divorced, and remarried individuals alike, the system builds a web of potential benefits designed to prevent catastrophic income drops after the major life events that tend to define a lifetime — retirement, disability, death, the end of a marriage.

As we move into later chapters, we'll connect these Social Security decisions to your broader retirement plan — how benefits interact with taxes, Medicare premiums, portfolio withdrawals, and annuity choices. But at the core of all of those chapters sits the exact insight you've worked through here: in a household, Social Security is never just about one person. It's a joint asset, a form of insurance, and a lifeline for whoever survives. Protecting that lifeline — especially the higher earner's benefit — may be one of the most important financial decisions you and your spouse will ever make together.

The Bottom Line

The moment you're married, Social Security stops being an individual decision and becomes a household one. Spousal benefits cap at 50% of the higher earner's PIA and never grow past your own FRA. Survivor benefits can reach 100% of what the higher earner was receiving — which is exactly why the higher earner's claiming age matters as much for their spouse's future as for their own. And if you've been divorced after a marriage lasting 10 years or more, you may have valuable options on an ex-spouse's record that most people never think to check.

KEY TAKEAWAYS

• Spousal benefits max out at 50% of the higher earner's PIA, claimed at your own FRA, and that benefit doesn't require you to have any work history of your own.

• You receive the greater of your own benefit or your spousal benefit — never both. Claiming your own benefit early permanently reduces the base that any future spousal "top-up" gets added to.

• Survivor benefits can reach up to 100% of what the deceased spouse was receiving — including any delayed retirement credits they earned. The higher earner's claiming decision sets the floor for the survivor's income, potentially for decades.

• Survivor benefits aren't subject to deemed filing, which means you can genuinely claim one type of benefit first and switch to the other later — a real, usable strategy most people never explore.

• Divorced after a marriage of 10+ years? You may be eligible for spousal or survivor benefits on your ex's record, with zero effect on what your ex or their current spouse receives. Remarriage before age 60 can end survivor eligibility on a prior spouse's record; remarriage after 60 generally preserves it.

Next up: how to turn everything you've learned so far into an actual lifetime-payout strategy — practical decision frameworks for singles and couples, plus real case studies showing how the math plays out differently depending on health, savings, and family circumstances.

Chapter 5: Maximize Lifetime Payouts: Practical Strategies that Work

Chapter at a Glance

What you'll learn in this chapter:

• Why delayed retirement credits function like longevity insurance rather than a gamble

• How to weigh immediate financial need against the long-term value of waiting, using a simple four-step framework

• How singles and couples should approach this decision differently — and why couples have more levers to pull

• Four real-world case studies showing how the same rules produce completely different "right answers" depending on health, savings, and family circumstances

Estimated reading time: 26 minutes

> ***FIELD NOTE*** *Every single one of the four people in this chapter's case studies had access to the exact same rules. Two of them benefited from delaying. One benefited from claiming early. One started with a plan and had to abandon it halfway through. None of them were wrong. That's the whole point of this chapter — there is no universal right answer, only a right process for finding yours.*

Most people think of Social Security as a simple on/off switch: you reach a certain age, you file, the checks start. In reality, you have far more control than that. The choices you make — especially around timing and coordination with a spouse — can shift your lifetime payout by tens, or even hundreds, of thousands of dollars. This chapter turns that messy, rule-heavy system into a practical toolkit you can actually use. Instead of fixating on finding a single "best age," you'll learn how to match your claiming strategy to your health, your budget, your work plans, and your broader retirement goals.

In earlier chapters, you saw how benefits get calculated and how they fit into your overall retirement income plan. Here, we layer strategy directly on top of that foundation. Think of this chapter as the playbook that helps you apply everything you've learned so far in real life, complete with step-by-step decision frameworks and case studies drawn from situations that closely mirror what real people actually face. The goal isn't squeezing every last dollar out of the system at any cost — it's maximizing your lifetime benefit while still sleeping well at night.

The right answer is almost never "always claim early" or "always wait until 70." Instead, we'll focus on how to weigh delayed retirement credits against immediate cash needs, how singles and couples can tailor their claiming patterns differently, and how real people in different circumstances balance longevity against income. By the end, you should be able to move from vague uncertainty — "I hope I'm doing this right" — to a clear, confident plan that actually fits you.

5.1 Strategies for Deciding When to Claim: Delay Credits vs. Immediate Needs

The first significant lever you control is timing. Claiming at 62 locks in the smallest monthly check you'll ever receive; waiting until 70 secures the largest. The years between those two ages are where strategy actually lives. To use that window wisely, you need to understand precisely what you're giving up, and precisely what you're gaining, for every single year you wait.

Understanding the Value of Delayed Retirement Credits

Once you reach your full retirement age — currently 66 to 67 for most people — Social Security starts rewarding your patience with delayed retirement credits. For anyone born in 1943 or later, your benefit rises by about 8% for each year you wait past FRA, up to age 70. This isn't a stock market projection, and it isn't a hopeful assumption. It's written into the law. Whether markets go up, down, or sideways that year, an 8% increase to your base benefit is locked in for life the moment you complete a full year of delay.

That 8% boost compounds on top of your Primary Insurance Amount, and is then multiplied over time by every future cost-of-living adjustment. Waiting from 67 to 70 doesn't just hand you three years of 8% increases — every future inflation adjustment from that point forward applies to a larger starting number. Over a retirement that stretches into your late 80s or 90s, that compounding difference becomes substantial. Delaying is one of the only ways to genuinely "buy" more guaranteed, inflation-adjusted lifetime income, and you accomplish it simply by waiting.

Of course, that extra income comes at a cost: you forgo checks throughout your 60s. The real question becomes, "Will I live long enough that the larger checks later more than make up for the checks I missed earlier?" If you live past your break-even age — covered in detail in Chapter 2 — the answer is usually yes. People in good health, with a family history of longevity, who don't need the money immediately, tend to be the best candidates for delaying. In effect, they're trading some early income for a form of longevity insurance: bigger, more secure cash flow in their 70s, 80s, and potentially their 90s.

Reframing delayed credits as insurance, rather than a gamble, genuinely changes the emotional calculation. You're not "betting that you'll live to 90." You're protecting yourself in case you do. That distinction matters enormously when you're weighing comfort in your 60s against security over a potentially very long life.

Evaluating Immediate Financial Needs and Health Factors

Not everyone can — or should — wait. Sometimes the reality of your situation makes claiming earlier the genuinely rational choice. Two major forces tend to push people in that direction: their current finances, and their health outlook.

If you're cash-strapped, carrying high-interest debt, or struggling to cover essential bills, waiting to claim may do more harm than good.

Using retirement savings to "bridge" all the way to 70 can be a smart move — but not if it forces you to raid funds in a way that leaves you dangerously exposed later. Likewise, if claiming at 62 lets you pay off a credit card charging 18% interest, that may genuinely be a better trade than waiting around for an 8% benefit increase. The math here isn't purely about Social Security — it's about your entire financial picture, all at once.

Health is the other major factor, and it deserves an honest look rather than wishful thinking. If you're dealing with serious medical conditions, a limited life expectancy, or a strong family history of early deaths, the odds of reaching your break-even age shrink considerably. In that case, starting earlier — even at 62 — can produce more total benefits over your actual lifetime. People often feel a strange guilt about claiming early, as if they're making a "bad" decision by doing so. But if your realistic lifespan is genuinely shorter, it can be entirely logical to collect more years of smaller checks rather than fewer years of larger checks you may never live to see.

You don't need a perfect prediction here — nobody has one. Take a sober, honest look at your health history, your lifestyle, and your family's patterns. Ask yourself whether it's reasonable to expect you, or your spouse, might live into your late 80s or beyond. If the answer is yes, the case for at least delaying until FRA — and possibly all the way to 70 — gets stronger. If the answer is no, early claiming may genuinely serve you better, especially if that extra income meaningfully improves your quality of life right now.

Step-by-Step Decision Framework

Because there are so many moving parts, it helps to follow a structured process rather than going with your gut. Use this framework as a checklist whenever you're deciding when to start.

Step 1: Calculate your break-even age. Estimate how different claiming ages compare in total dollars over your lifetime — the age at which total benefits from claiming later finally catch up to the total you'd have collected by claiming earlier. You're essentially asking: "If I claim at 62 versus 70, at what age does the total from waiting surpass the total from starting early?" Often, that age falls somewhere in your late 70s or early 80s. Knowing that target lets you connect the math directly to your own longevity expectations.

Step 2: Analyze your immediate income needs versus future benefits. Take a hard look at your cash flow. What are your essential monthly expenses? What income do you already have — from work, pensions, savings, or other sources? Could you cover your needs without Social Security for a few more years, maybe by drawing modestly from a 401(k) or IRA? Or would delaying force you into high-interest debt or cutting necessities? A realistic budget clarifies exactly how much flexibility you actually have.

Step 3: Weigh personal factors such as other income sources and retirement assets. Layer in what you learned in earlier chapters about your total retirement plan. Substantial savings, a pension, or part-time income might let you treat Social Security as a "backstop" you allow to grow undisturbed. If Social Security represents the bulk of your lifetime income, the choice becomes considerably more consequential. Consider how taxes, work plans, and investment risk interact with your claiming age — sometimes spending a bit more from investments early lets you lock in a far more secure guaranteed benefit later.

Step 4: Choose the claiming age that balances financial security and peace of mind. Finally, recognize this isn't purely a spreadsheet problem. The best strategy is the one you can actually live with. If delaying until 70 gives you genuine anxiety about "running out of money" in your 60s, a compromise — claiming at 66 or 67 instead of either extreme — might be exactly right. If knowing you've maximized survivor benefits, or protected yourself against a very long life, helps you sleep soundly, you may be perfectly comfortable delaying further. Aim for an age that preserves your dignity and independence today, while still protecting you from hardship decades from now.

This decision framework connects directly to the principles you explored earlier in the book when building your retirement income plan: weighing trade-offs, aligning numbers with your actual values, and treating Social Security as one essential piece of a much larger puzzle.

Planning for Flexibility: The Role of Social Security's Withdrawal Options

Part of why the claiming decision feels so heavy is that people assume it's entirely irreversible. In reality, Social Security offers a couple of genuine "do-over" tools — limited, and with strings attached, but real. Knowing about these options can ease the pressure you feel before you file.

The first is the withdrawal option. Start receiving benefits, and then within 12 months realize you made a mistake — maybe you went back to work, inherited assets, or simply learned more about delayed credits — and you can file a formal withdrawal of your application. You'll need to repay every benefit you received, plus any benefits paid to a spouse or dependent on your record. Once that's done, it's treated as if you never claimed at all. Your future benefit gets recalculated as though you had waited the entire time, and you can reapply later for a higher amount.

This "reset button" can only be used once in your lifetime, and not everyone will have the means or the desire to repay what they've already collected. Still, simply knowing it exists can lower the psychological stakes of your initial decision. If your situation changes dramatically in that first year, you're not locked forever into your first choice.

A second form of flexibility kicks in once you reach full retirement age. At that point, if you're already collecting, you can suspend your benefit. You don't have to repay anything you've received, but your checks stop — as will any spousal benefits paid on your record, though not benefits paid to an ex-spouse — and you start earning delayed retirement credits again, up to age 70. This can be genuinely useful if you claimed earlier than you now wish you had, and later discover you can afford to go without the income for a while.

Both of these options reinforce an important point: claiming isn't always a perfect, one-and-done moment. Your health can change. Your work plans can shift. Markets can surprise you. Building awareness of the withdrawal and suspension rules into your strategy lets you be a little bolder when the facts genuinely justify it, knowing you have at least some room to adjust course later.

5.2 Tailoring Claiming Patterns for Singles and Couples

Timing strategies become even more interesting — and more powerful — once you layer in personal circumstances like marital status. Singles and couples face genuinely different trade-offs and opportunities. The system was designed not just to support individual workers, but to protect households, particularly surviving spouses. Understanding those dynamics lets you shape a true household plan, rather than thinking about each person's benefit in isolation.

Singles: Focusing on Maximizing Individual Benefits

If you're single, divorced without qualifying for spousal benefits, or widowed but ultimately relying on your own retirement benefit, your strategy is simpler in one specific way: you're planning only for yourself. The main question becomes how to balance the value of a higher monthly check later against your need for income — and your health outlook — today.

For a lot of healthy singles, especially anyone expecting a long retirement, delaying can be particularly valuable. You don't have a spouse to fall back on if you live longer than expected. That means you're personally exposed to longevity risk — the chance you might outlive your savings. In that context, waiting until 70 often maximizes lifetime payouts, because you're statistically more likely to reach or exceed the break-even age where higher monthly checks catch up to the foregone early payments.

On the other hand, some singles have limited savings or lower lifetime earnings. If Social Security is going to be your primary income source, early claiming may genuinely be necessary just to maintain a basic standard of living. There's no virtue in waiting so long that you struggle unnecessarily through your 60s. The art lies in finding a claiming age that keeps you solvent now, while still providing as much long-term protection as your situation realistically allows. The step-by-step framework from earlier in this chapter matters especially here, because you're making this decision without the backstop of a spouse's benefit behind you.

Married Couples: Coordinating to Protect Household Income

For couples, the picture gets more complex — but also more promising. You have two earnings records, two potential retirement benefits, possible spousal benefits, and survivor benefits all in play simultaneously. Coordinate these wisely and you can significantly increase the guaranteed income flowing into your household over time.

One powerful guiding principle: in many couples, the higher earner's benefit is effectively a "joint and survivor" benefit. It pays as long as that person is alive, and then frequently becomes the surviving spouse's benefit for the rest of their life too. This creates a strong case for the higher earner to delay claiming — sometimes all the way to 70 — to maximize not just their own income, but the survivor benefit waiting down the road.

Meanwhile, the lower-earning spouse can often claim earlier, bringing some income into the household while the higher earner waits. This "team strategy" balances cash flow against long-term optimization. The lower earner might file at 62 or their own FRA, providing a base stream of income that supports the couple, reduces pressure on investments, and makes it considerably easier for the higher earner to actually follow through on delaying.

Spousal benefits layer on top of this. If one spouse's own benefit is modest, they may be eligible for up to 50% of the higher earner's FRA benefit as a spousal benefit once both are claiming. Used thoughtfully, this creates a laddered claiming approach: the lower earner files first on their own record, then steps up to a higher spousal amount once the higher earner claims, if that amount turns out to be available. The rules around "deemed filing" have tightened for newer cohorts, as covered in Chapter 4, but the basic coordinating principle still holds: time your claims to support today's needs while protecting whichever spouse lives the longest.

Considering Age Differences and Survivor Benefits in Couples

Age gaps complicate the picture further, but they also highlight the protective power of delaying the higher earner's benefit. When one spouse is significantly younger, the odds are high that the younger spouse will spend many years as a survivor. The benefit they receive during those years is usually based on what the higher earner was receiving at the time of death, including any delayed retirement credits already earned.

Every year the higher earner delays past their FRA doesn't just boost their own monthly income — it potentially increases what the younger survivor will collect for the rest of their life too. In couples with large age gaps, it's often especially important for the higher earner to wait as long as health and finances allow. Maximizing that top-line benefit can shield the surviving spouse from inflation, market downturns, and the loss of one Social Security check the moment the first spouse dies.

When mapping this out, picture household income across three distinct phases: while both spouses are working, while both are retired, and after one spouse has died. Optimize only for the middle phase, and you can inadvertently leave the surviving spouse short later. A genuinely strong strategy makes sure survivor benefits are robust enough to cover essential expenses, recognizing the widowed spouse will have one less Social Security check, and likely lower overall household income, going forward.

Age differences also affect the sequencing of claims. The older spouse might claim earlier to provide near-term income, while the younger spouse — if they're the higher earner — delays claiming to grow that eventual survivor benefit. Or the younger, lower earner might claim first if that better fits their needs. The key is never treating each person's claim in isolation, but choreographing them together with survivor rules firmly in mind.

Impact of Divorce or Widowhood on Claiming Patterns

Life doesn't always follow the "standard" script. Divorce, widowhood, and remarriage can all reshuffle your menu of Social Security options — and if you're not paying attention, you can easily leave money on the table.

If you're divorced, you may still qualify for benefits based on your ex-spouse's record, provided the marriage lasted at least 10 consecutive years, you're currently unmarried (or your later marriages have ended), and both of you are at least 62. Under these rules, you may be entitled to a spousal benefit of up to 50% of your ex's FRA benefit, if that's higher than what you'd receive on your own record. You don't get both — Social Security simply pays whichever is higher — and your claim doesn't reduce what your ex, or their current spouse, can receive.

For divorced individuals, timing matters in a specific way. Because divorced spousal benefits max out at full retirement age and don't earn delayed credits beyond that point, there's usually no advantage to waiting past FRA to claim them, if they're already higher than your own benefit. Once you reach FRA, you typically want to start them, assuming you're not still working at a level that would trigger earnings-related reductions.

Widows and widowers face a different set of options entirely. Survivor benefits can begin as early as 60 (or 50 if disabled), and can sometimes exceed the survivor's own retirement benefit. You might choose to start with a survivor benefit and switch to your own retirement benefit at 70, letting it grow with delayed credits in the meantime. Or you might claim your own reduced benefit early and switch to a full survivor benefit at your own full retirement age, since survivor benefits themselves don't increase further beyond that point. The best path depends on which benefit will eventually be larger, and how your ages and earnings line up against each other.

These rules can feel technical on the page, but the underlying principle is simple: divorced and widowed individuals often have more than one potential benefit stream, and you may be able to sequence them deliberately over time, rather than being forced into a single, irreversible choice. Understanding these nuances, and coordinating them with your overall retirement plan, gives you a genuinely better shot at maximizing lifetime income, even after major life transitions reshape your circumstances.

5.3 Real-World Walkthroughs: Income and Longevity Trade-Offs

All the theory in the world doesn't help much if you can't see how it actually plays out for real people. In this section, we'll walk through four illustrative case studies. The numbers are simplified and hypothetical, but the trade-offs mirror what a lot of readers will face. As you read, mentally substitute your own ages, incomes, and health outlook. The goal isn't copying these strategies exactly — it's recognizing patterns you can adapt to your own life.

Case Study 1: Healthy Retiree Choosing Between Age 62 and 70

Meet Carol, a 62-year-old single woman who's worked consistently for over 35 years. Her FRA is 67, and if she waits until then, she's projected to receive a $2,000 monthly benefit. Claim now at 62 and her check drops by about 30%, to roughly $1,400 a month. Wait until 70 instead, and delayed retirement credits boost her benefit by 24% above her FRA amount, landing her around $2,480 a month.

At first glance, $1,400 a month starting right now feels tempting. Carol could cover a good chunk of her expenses without drawing too heavily on her savings. But her health is excellent, she enjoys a balanced lifestyle, and both her parents lived into their late 80s and 90s. She reasonably expects a long retirement — possibly three decades or more.

When Carol estimates her break-even age between 62 and 70, she finds that if she lives into her early 80s, the higher benefit from waiting will yield more total dollars than starting early. Past that point, every additional year she lives widens the gap in favor of the delayed strategy. And because the $2,480 benefit is indexed for inflation, every future cost-of-living adjustment is worth more in real dollars than it would be on the smaller check.

Carol looks at her budget and realizes she could bridge the gap by working part-time for a few more years, combined with modest withdrawals from her retirement accounts. That would let her delay claiming until at least 67, and possibly all the way to 70. For someone in her position — healthy, with some savings, a good chance of living past the break-even age — waiting appears to maximize not just her lifetime income, but her overall sense of security later in life.

If Carol's health were genuinely uncertain, though, this balance would shift. In that alternative scenario, claiming at 62 could easily produce more total income over a shorter lifetime, even with the lower monthly amount. The key point: the right choice depends entirely on her specific life expectancy and resources — not on a generic rule that says everyone should always delay, or everyone should always claim early.

Case Study 2: Single Parent with Limited Retirement Savings

Now consider Miguel, a 63-year-old single father whose children are grown. He spent years juggling work and caregiving, which limited how much he could save and kept his earnings modest throughout. His FRA is 67, with a projected benefit of $1,800 a month. Claim at 63 and his benefit drops to around $1,440. Wait until 70 and he'd receive roughly $2,232 a month.

Miguel's challenge is simpler on paper than it is in real life: he needs the income. His job recently ended, his savings are minimal, and he has no pension. He's found occasional part-time work, but not enough to comfortably cover rent, food, and healthcare. Waiting until 70 feels close to impossible — he worries he'd deplete what little savings he has and end up racking up credit card debt in the meantime.

This is exactly where the tension between urgent needs and delayed credits becomes very real. Miguel could claim now at 63, lock in $1,440, and breathe a little easier about his monthly bills. But he'd also be giving up three years of potential 8% increases between 67 and 70 — increases that could matter enormously later, if he lives longer than he currently expects. He feels genuinely torn between surviving the next few years and protecting himself at 80 or 85.

To navigate this, Miguel starts by tightening his budget and exploring supplemental strategies. He looks into more stable part-time work, considers a roommate to share housing costs, and checks into local support programs that could reduce his expenses. With some effort, he realizes he might be able to delay claiming until at least 65 or 66, even if 70 isn't realistic for him. That compromise could give him a higher base benefit without forcing severe hardship right now.

He also considers a phased approach: claiming at 65 instead of 63, which buys him time to pay down some debt and strengthen his savings first. In the meantime, he leans on part-time earnings and small, planned withdrawals from his retirement account as a short-term bridge. It's not a perfect solution — but it acknowledges that for a lot of people with limited savings, the real decision isn't between ideal and ideal. It's between "adequate now, vulnerable later" and "tight now, safer later."

Miguel's situation underscores something crucial: maximizing lifetime payouts matters, but so does getting through the present without undue stress or deprivation. Sometimes, especially for those with modest means, you have to accept some loss in theoretical lifetime benefit in exchange for practical stability today. The trick is being intentional about that trade-off, rather than drifting into it by default.

Case Study 3: Married Couple with a Significant Age Gap

Our third example shows how couples can coordinate claims to support income now while maximizing survivor protection later. Meet Denise, 66, and her husband Aaron, 58. Denise is the higher earner, with a FRA benefit of $2,400 a month. Aaron's own benefit at his FRA (67) will be $1,200 a month. They have some savings, but lean heavily on Social Security in their overall planning.

Because Denise is older and the higher earner, her benefit will likely form the backbone of their retirement income for decades — and will eventually become Aaron's survivor benefit if she dies first. The couple wants income relatively soon, since Denise is ready to stop working, but they're also aware that Aaron might spend 20 or 30 years as a widower down the line.

One common approach in this kind of situation is for the older spouse to claim early and bring in cash right away. In Denise's case, though, that would reduce the very benefit Aaron will eventually depend on as a survivor. Instead, they consider a different strategy: Denise delays claiming as long as possible, ideally until 70, to maximize both her own income and Aaron's eventual survivor benefit. Meanwhile, they look for other ways to generate near-term cash flow.

Because Aaron is younger and still working part-time, they decide he'll keep earning for several more years while Denise delays. When Aaron eventually stops working around 65, he can claim his own benefit to start a moderate stream of household income. If Denise is still waiting at that point, Aaron's benefit helps bridge the gap, reducing how heavily they need to draw from savings.

Once Denise reaches 70 and claims, her much larger benefit kicks in, and Aaron — if his own benefit is lower than half of hers — may become eligible for a higher spousal amount. Over time, as they age, the combination of Denise's maximized benefit and Aaron's own or spousal benefit creates a strong income floor for the household. If Denise dies first, Aaron steps up to her full benefit as a survivor. Because she delayed, that survivor check is as large as it can possibly be — protecting him through what could be a very long remaining lifetime.

They make a point of revisiting this plan regularly, exactly as discussed in earlier chapters. If health or income changes, they can adjust their claiming dates within the flexibility the rules allow. The big lesson here: for couples with significant age gaps, it often makes more sense to think less about the earliest years of retirement, and more about what income will look like 10, 20, or even 30 years down the line — particularly for the younger spouse.

Case Study 4: Retiree Facing Unexpected Health Decline

Finally, consider James, age 69, who decided at 66 to delay his Social Security until 70. His FRA benefit is $2,100 a month, and by 70 it would reach around $2,604 with delayed credits factored in. At 66, James was in excellent health, had solid savings, and enjoyed his consulting work. Delaying seemed like an obvious win.

Two years later, things look different. James has been diagnosed with a serious illness, and his doctors suggest his life expectancy may be considerably shorter than he once thought. He's also stopped working, and his healthcare and living expenses have risen. Suddenly, the logic of delaying until 70 feels far less obvious. Should he keep waiting to maximize a benefit he might only collect for a few years — or claim now and start drawing income while he still feels relatively well?

Because James is already past his full retirement age, he has significant flexibility here. He can claim immediately at 69, locking in a benefit that's already higher than his FRA amount, thanks to the delayed credits he's already earned. Alternatively, if his health unexpectedly improved or his finances shifted, he could even suspend his benefit after starting, letting credits resume in the background.

James and his advisor revisit his overall plan. They model total lifetime benefits under several scenarios, weighing his actual priorities: enjoying time with family now, covering rising medical costs, and avoiding unnecessary stress. Given his shortened life expectancy, claiming right away at 69 appears to provide more genuine value than squeezing out one more year of credits in hopes of a higher check at 70. The marginal increase from waiting no longer compensates for the real risk that he might not live long enough to benefit from it.

They also note that, had he claimed earlier in life, the 12-month withdrawal option could have given him a reset. Since he delayed from the very beginning, that particular tool isn't something he needs. Still, knowing that withdrawal and suspension options exist reinforces a broader lesson running through this entire chapter: your strategy shouldn't be static. It should evolve as your health, finances, and priorities evolve too.

James's case highlights a theme that runs through this whole chapter, and really the whole book: the "optimal" claiming strategy isn't about squeezing every possible dollar out of the system in some abstract sense. It's about matching the rules and the available tools to the actual life you end up living — not just the one you imagined when you first retired. Revisiting your decisions regularly, in connection with the holistic planning framework from earlier chapters, is what lets you pivot when life genuinely surprises you.

Taken together, these four strategies and examples show that maximizing lifetime Social Security payouts is less about a single magic trick, and far more about a series of thoughtful, well-timed moves. You weigh delayed credits against immediate needs, coordinate benefits within a household, respect the realities of health, work, and savings, and stay flexible enough to adjust when circumstances change. In the chapters that follow, you'll build on this foundation by exploring how to integrate these claiming decisions with tax planning, investment withdrawal strategies, and legacy goals — transforming Social Security from a standalone program into a fully integrated part of your retirement life.

The Bottom Line

There's no single magic claiming age that works for everyone — there's only a process for finding the age that works for you. Run your break-even calculation. Be honest about your immediate cash needs and your health outlook. If you're married, coordinate your decision with your spouse rather than making two separate choices. And remember that the decision, while important, isn't entirely set in stone — withdrawal and suspension options exist if your circumstances change.

KEY TAKEAWAYS

- Delayed retirement credits add roughly 8% per year to your benefit between FRA and age 70 — a guaranteed, inflation-adjusted increase that's hard to replicate anywhere else in your financial life.
- Reframe delayed claiming as longevity insurance, not a gamble. You're not betting you'll live to 90 — you're protecting yourself in case you do.
- Genuine financial need and serious health concerns are legitimate reasons to claim early. The mistake isn't claiming early — it's claiming early without running the numbers first.
- Singles carry their own longevity risk with no spousal backstop, which often strengthens the case for delaying if health allows. Couples have more levers: the lower earner can claim early for cash flow while the higher earner delays to protect the eventual survivor.
- You have limited but real flexibility after filing — a 12-month withdrawal option, and the ability to suspend benefits after FRA. Your claiming decision doesn't have to be perfect on day one; it has to be reasonable, and revisited as life changes.

Next up: how Social Security actually gets taxed — why some retirees pay tax on up to 85% of their benefit while others pay nothing, and the specific strategies that keep more of your check in your own pocket.

Chapter 6: Taxes and Social Security: Keep More of What You Earn

Chapter at a Glance

What you'll learn in this chapter:

• What "provisional income" actually is, and why it — not your benefit amount — decides how much of your check gets taxed

• The exact thresholds that determine whether you pay tax on 0%, 50%, or 85% of your Social Security benefit

• Why municipal bond interest, of all things, can quietly push more of your benefit into the taxable zone

• Practical strategies — Roth conversions, withdrawal timing, charitable distributions — that can meaningfully reduce what you owe over a 20-year retirement

Estimated reading time: 23 minutes

> ***FIELD NOTE*** *I watched a client find out, the hard way, that an extra $1,000 IRA withdrawal had actually cost him $1,850 in taxable income for the year — not $1,000. He hadn't done anything wrong. He just didn't know that pulling more from his IRA also dragged more of his Social Security into the taxable zone. That single conversation is most of why this chapter exists.*

Most people expect Social Security to feel like a reward after decades of work — a dependable check landing in their account every month, full stop. What often comes as a genuinely rude surprise is that, for a lot of retirees, a slice of that check goes right back out the door in federal income tax. The system is confusing, the rules feel buried inside IRS worksheets, and it's remarkably easy to make decisions — about when to claim, how much to withdraw from savings, how to invest — that unintentionally bump you into a higher tax bill without you ever realizing it happened.

This chapter exists to remove that surprise entirely. By the time you finish it, you'll understand exactly how the government decides whether your Social Security is taxable, why some retirees pay tax on up to 85% of their benefit while others pay nothing at all, and what you can actually do — before and after you claim — to keep more of what you've earned. We'll work through the concept of "provisional income," walk through realistic examples, and then connect those concepts to practical strategies: timing your withdrawals, using Roth accounts wisely, choosing which assets to spend first, and deciding whether Roth conversions or charitable tools belong in your own plan.

In earlier chapters, you learned how to estimate your benefits, how different claiming ages affect your monthly check, and how to coordinate spousal and survivor benefits. Taxes are the next layer on top of all of that. Think of this chapter as the bridge between those claiming decisions and the broader retirement plan you'll continue building in later chapters — where we'll pull investments, healthcare, estate planning, and income strategy into one integrated picture. For now, we're zooming in specifically on the tax side of Social Security, because the gap between a tax-savvy plan and a tax-blind one can easily add up to tens of thousands of dollars over a long retirement.

6.1 How Social Security Benefits Are Taxed: Provisional Income and Thresholds

To understand Social Security taxation, you need exactly one term: provisional income. The IRS doesn't simply look at your benefit in isolation — it considers your total financial picture, and uses provisional income as the measuring stick that determines how much of your Social Security is actually taxable.

Provisional income isn't a number you'll find printed anywhere on your tax return, but it drives the entire calculation behind the scenes. The IRS uses it because Social Security is meant to function as a baseline of support. If you have little or no other income, your benefits stay generally tax-free. As your other income grows, the IRS phases in taxation on a growing portion of your Social Security — up to a maximum of 85%.

That phrase matters enormously: up to 85% of your benefit can become taxable income. Your benefits are never taxed at an 85% rate. Up to 85% of what you receive gets included in your taxable income and then taxed at your normal rates — a meaningfully different thing, and a distinction that trips up almost everyone the first time they hear it.

Definition of Provisional Income

Provisional income follows a specific formula. You calculate it by adding three components together:

1. Your adjusted gross income (AGI), not counting Social Security.

2. Any tax-exempt interest you receive — municipal bond interest, for example.

3. One-half of your annual Social Security benefits.

In plain language: provisional income equals your AGI (without Social Security) plus tax-exempt interest plus half your Social Security benefits.

Adjusted gross income covers wages, self-employment income, traditional IRA and 401(k) distributions, pension payments, taxable interest, dividends, capital gains, and most other taxable income sources. It does not include qualified withdrawals from Roth IRAs or Roth 401(k)s, and it doesn't include Social Security itself — that gets added back separately, at half value, in step three.

The "tax-exempt interest" add-back is one of the biggest surprises for new retirees. You might have spent years carefully building a municipal bond ladder specifically because the interest was exempt from federal income tax. For ordinary tax purposes, it still is. But for the specific purpose of calculating Social Security taxation, that interest still counts toward provisional income. The IRS isn't taxing the interest directly — it's using it to decide how much of your Social Security becomes taxable instead. A subtle distinction, but a costly one if you don't see it coming.

Adding in half of your Social Security benefits might look arbitrary at first glance, but it's genuinely at the core of how this entire system works. Receive more in benefits, or pair those benefits with high other income, and more of your Social Security is likely to be taxed – though never more than 85%, no matter how high your other income climbs.

You won't see "provisional income" sitting on a specific line of Form 1040. Instead, the IRS folds the calculation into a worksheet that ultimately determines the taxable portion you transfer onto your return. Still, running the formula yourself each year – even with a simple spreadsheet – lets you project what's coming well before tax season actually arrives.

Income Thresholds That Trigger Taxation

Once you have your provisional income figure, the next step is comparing it against the IRS thresholds. Unlike the regular tax brackets, which get updated annually for inflation, these particular thresholds were set back in the 1980s and 1990s and have never been indexed since. That means more people get pulled into paying tax on their benefits over time, simply because wages and the cost of living have risen while these specific numbers have stayed completely frozen.

For individuals filing as single, head of household, or qualifying widow(er):

• Below $25,000 in provisional income: your Social Security benefits are generally tax-free at the federal level.

• Between $25,000 and $34,000: up to 50% of your benefits may become taxable.

• Above $34,000: up to 85% of your benefits may be taxable.

For married couples filing jointly, the thresholds run higher:

• Below $32,000 in provisional income: benefits are usually tax-free.

• Between $32,000 and $44,000: up to 50% of benefits may be taxable.

• Above $44,000: up to 85% of benefits may be taxable.

These ranges set the maximum share of your benefit that can be included in taxable income. The actual dollar amount gets worked out through stepwise formulas inside the IRS worksheet, but for planning purposes, thinking in tiers gets you most of the way there. Sit just over the lower threshold and only a small portion of your benefit might end up taxable. Climb higher and more of your benefit gets pulled in, until you hit the point where 85% of your annual benefit is taxable every single year going forward.

Here's the planning insight that matters most: once you're in the "up to 85%" zone, additional income can create a higher marginal tax rate than you'd expect from your bracket alone. An extra $1,000 of IRA withdrawals doesn't just get taxed on its own — it can also cause an additional $850 of your Social Security to become taxable at the same time. In that situation, you're effectively paying tax on $1,850, not just on the $1,000 you actually withdrew. This is exactly why thoughtful income management in retirement can save real, substantial money over time — it's not a minor optimization, it's often the single biggest lever available to you.

Married Couples' Different Thresholds

For married couples filing jointly, the $32,000 and $44,000 thresholds reflect a basic recognition that two people typically need more income than one. In practice, this means couples can often earn more from pensions, IRAs, or part-time work before any of their Social Security becomes taxable at all.

This difference matters in several specific ways. First, it can influence your choice of filing status. Most married retirees file jointly, but in rare situations — particularly after separation or a late-life divorce in progress — filing separately comes into consideration. Under the Social Security tax rules, married filing separately is almost always the most disadvantageous status available. In many cases, if you lived with your spouse at any point during the year and then file separately, up to 85% of your benefits may become taxable regardless of your actual provisional income. That harsh result is exactly why it's worth thinking carefully, and getting advice, before choosing "married filing separately" in retirement.

Second, couples need to think about how their combined income interacts with these thresholds. You don't get a separate $25,000 or $32,000 threshold for each spouse individually – the IRS pools your household income together. If one spouse keeps working while the other has already claimed Social Security, that wage income, combined with any joint IRA withdrawals, can push the couple into the 50% or 85% zones faster than either spouse might expect on their own.

Third, these thresholds interact directly with the claiming decisions covered in Chapter 5. If the higher-earning spouse delays claiming until 70 while the lower earner claims earlier, the couple's provisional income pattern shifts meaningfully over time. The early years might feature more savings withdrawals and less Social Security income. The later years might bring larger benefits alongside fewer IRA withdrawals, if balances have already been drawn down. Coordinating those patterns with the tax thresholds is genuinely one of the levers you can pull to reduce lifetime taxes – not an afterthought, but part of the original claiming strategy itself.

Impact of Other Income Types

Almost every other source of retirement income – with the notable exception of Roth withdrawals and a few specialized benefits – affects provisional income, and therefore Social Security taxation. Here are the most common culprits:

- Wages and self-employment earnings from part-time work.
- Pensions from former employers.
- Distributions from traditional IRAs, 401(k)s, 403(b)s, and similar plans.
- Interest from bank accounts, CDs, and bonds.
- Dividends from stocks and mutual funds.
- Capital gains when you sell investments for more than you paid.
- Tax-exempt municipal bond interest.

Each dollar from these sources increases your AGI (or, in the case of municipal bonds, gets added back separately), which raises your provisional income. That can move you out of the no-tax zone and into the 50% zone, or out of the 50% zone and into the 85% zone, depending on where you started.

Roth IRA and Roth 401(k) qualified withdrawals are the important exception worth remembering. As long as you meet the age and holding-period rules, those withdrawals never appear in your AGI and never get added back for provisional income purposes. They give you genuinely tax-free cash that doesn't trigger any additional taxation on your Social Security — which is exactly why Roth accounts get so much attention in retirement income planning, and why we'll return to them shortly.

Even "nontaxable" items can matter here in ways that surprise people. A lot of retirees think of municipal bond interest as essentially invisible to the IRS, but it's very much visible in this specific context. Holding large amounts of tax-exempt bonds in a taxable account can unintentionally push you into higher Social Security taxation — a genuinely ironic outcome for investors who built that portfolio specifically chasing tax efficiency.

All of this points toward one big-picture conclusion: you can't look at Social Security taxation in isolation. It's tied directly to your entire income design — how much you withdraw from which accounts, when you take pension income, whether you sell appreciated investments, and how you've structured your assets between traditional and Roth accounts. The rest of this chapter is devoted to showing you exactly how to use that fact to your advantage, rather than letting it work against you by accident.

6.2 Tax-Reduction Strategies for Retirees

Once you understand how provisional income and the thresholds actually work, the next step is using that knowledge to shape your retirement decisions deliberately. You can't control every variable — markets fluctuate, health changes, tax laws evolve over time — but you do have meaningful levers available to manage how much tax you pay on your Social Security each year.

The strategies in this section center on timing and balance: timing your withdrawals, timing your claim, and balancing which accounts you draw from. They connect directly to the broader retirement income planning you'll explore later in this book, where we look at building a sustainable "paycheck" from your savings. Here, we're focused specifically on the tax angle.

Timing Your Withdrawals Wisely

When you retire, you likely have a mix of accounts: traditional IRAs and 401(k)s, Roth accounts, and taxable brokerage accounts. Every withdrawal decision you make touches your provisional income in some way.

One powerful choice is exactly when you start taking distributions from traditional, tax-deferred accounts, relative to when you claim Social Security. For a lot of people, there's a genuine "gap period" between the day they stop full-time work and the day they actually claim benefits. During those years, provisional income may be relatively low, especially if pensions and required minimum distributions (RMDs) haven't started yet.

In that gap, you might intentionally withdraw more from traditional accounts than you strictly need, taking advantage of your temporarily lower tax bracket. Those withdrawals raise your current taxable income, but since you haven't claimed Social Security yet, they don't push any additional benefits into taxation. At the same time, you're shrinking the size of your traditional accounts, which reduces RMDs later — right when you'll likely be receiving Social Security and may already be at risk of sitting in the 85% zone.

Alternatively, you might choose to start Social Security earlier and limit IRA withdrawals for a few years instead. This can provide more guaranteed income and preserve your portfolio, but it may also expose more of your benefit to tax if you end up needing larger IRA withdrawals later, right when they coincide with higher Social Security income. The better choice depends on your life expectancy, your investment mix, your risk tolerance, and your overall priorities. The point isn't that there's one universally "right" answer — it's that you should make a conscious decision instead of drifting into a default pattern by accident.

Even after you've started both Social Security and RMDs, timing still matters. You may want to bunch certain types of income — business-sale proceeds, for example — into particular years, then pull back on other taxable withdrawals in the years around it. By projecting your provisional income across several years rather than just the current one, you can avoid repeatedly hitting the steepest part of the Social Security tax slope, year after year, without realizing it.

Taking Advantage of Lower Income Years

Retirement income is rarely perfectly consistent. You might have a year when you stop working mid-year, another when significant medical expenses or large itemized deductions show up, and yet another when a spouse retires later than you did. These natural dips in income present genuine opportunities, if you're watching for them.

During years when your provisional income is lower — either before claiming Social Security, or while only one spouse is collecting — you can:

• Realize more long-term capital gains at favorable rates.

• Increase IRA withdrawals voluntarily, even above any required minimum distribution, to fill up lower tax brackets while they're available.

• Execute partial Roth conversions (more on this shortly).

• Delay claiming Social Security for another year, which both increases your future benefit and avoids adding half of that benefit to provisional income for the current year.

Even once you're already receiving Social Security, low-income years can still work in your favor. Maybe you have a year without significant capital gains, or your deductible expenses are temporarily elevated. In those years, an extra $5,000 or $10,000 of IRA distributions might only slightly increase your provisional income — but it could prevent you from being pushed into a higher tax bracket, or losing valuable tax credits, later once RMDs become mandatory and unavoidable.

This kind of multi-year thinking separates reactive filers from proactive planners. Instead of asking every December, "What can I do before year-end?", step back and look at the next five or ten years of likely income, Social Security claiming ages, and RMD schedules all at once. You'll see pockets of low income where it makes sense to accelerate taxable income, and pockets of high income where you genuinely want to minimize it. This echoes exactly what you learned in earlier chapters about optimizing when to claim Social Security – except now you're layering in tax brackets and provisional income thresholds as additional guideposts on top of the timing decision itself.

Using Tax-Advantaged Accounts

Roth accounts are among the most flexible tools available for managing Social Security taxation, precisely because qualified withdrawals don't count toward provisional income at all. If you hold both traditional and Roth savings, you can blend your withdrawals to keep provisional income inside a more favorable range, year by year.

Picture a simple example: you're a single retiree receiving $30,000 a year in Social Security. Half of that, $15,000, automatically feeds into your provisional income calculation. If you also need $25,000 from savings to support your lifestyle, you could:

- Take the entire $25,000 from a traditional IRA, pushing your provisional income high enough that up to 85% of your Social Security becomes taxable, or

- Take $10,000 from a traditional IRA and $15,000 from a Roth IRA, which may keep you in the 50% zone or even below it, depending on your other income.

Over time, this kind of blended approach can save you thousands of dollars in federal income tax, while giving you the flexibility to handle unexpected expenses without blowing up your tax picture. If a major home repair hits in a year when you're already close to the 85% threshold, you might draw more heavily from Roth accounts or cash reserves instead, specifically to avoid an expensive spike in provisional income that year.

Planning for Roth accounts genuinely needs to start well before retirement. That might mean contributing directly if you qualify, using Roth options inside your workplace plan, or running Roth conversions through your 50s and 60s. Earlier chapters on saving strategies and account types laid the groundwork for this; this chapter shows you one of the key payoffs – the ability to meet spending needs without constantly dragging more of your Social Security into higher taxation.

Managing Investment Income

Investment income is another lever you can adjust, within limits, to manage your provisional income. Capital gains, dividends, and interest all flow through AGI and can increase the share of Social Security that becomes taxable — but there are several tactics worth considering here.

First, place tax-inefficient investments inside tax-advantaged accounts whenever possible. Hold bond funds or high-dividend stocks inside an IRA, and the interest and dividends never show up in your current AGI. You'll eventually pay tax when you withdraw, but at that point you control the timing and the amount entirely. Meanwhile, you can hold more tax-efficient index funds or low-turnover individual stocks in your taxable accounts, where you decide exactly when to realize gains.

Second, pay close attention to capital gains timing. Selling appreciated investments in a year when you're already near the 85% provisional income threshold can be genuinely costly — you might get pushed into higher ordinary brackets, and more of your Social Security may become taxable at the exact same time. Realizing gains in a year when your other income is lower, by contrast, often means a much smaller impact on your Social Security, and in some cases, long-term capital gains may even be taxed at 0%.

Third, use tax-loss harvesting to offset gains where you can. If you need to sell winners, look for underperforming investments to sell at a loss in the same calendar year. The losses offset your gains dollar for dollar, and a modest amount of leftover losses can even offset ordinary income. This strategy doesn't change your provisional income directly, since both the gains and losses flow through AGI either way — but it helps manage your overall tax bill, and lets you rebalance your portfolio with considerably less tax drag along the way.

Because investment income interacts so closely with portfolio needs, risk tolerance, and the tax rules, it's usually wise to bring in a tax professional or financial planner before making any significant moves. They can run projections showing not just the immediate tax impact of a decision, but how it ripples into your Social Security taxation in future years too.

6.3 Roth Conversions and Other Planning Opportunities

Roth conversions deserve their own dedicated spotlight, because they sit right at the intersection of several themes running through this book: building flexible income streams, managing required minimum distributions, and controlling Social Security taxation across many years at once. Other tools — charitable distributions, carefully chosen annuities — play supporting roles, but can be genuinely powerful in the right circumstances too.

What Is a Roth Conversion?

A Roth conversion is the process of moving money from a pre-tax retirement account — a traditional IRA or 401(k) — into a Roth IRA. When you convert, the amount you move is treated as taxable income for that year. You pay the income tax now, in exchange for three significant benefits later:

• Future qualified withdrawals from the Roth are completely tax-free.

• Roth balances aren't subject to required minimum distributions during your lifetime.

• Roth withdrawals never count toward provisional income, and therefore never increase the taxation of your Social Security.

Think of a Roth conversion as prepaying tax on a slice of your retirement savings at today's rates, in exchange for shielding future growth and withdrawals from taxation entirely. The trade-off is the immediate tax cost, weighed against long-term flexibility and potentially lower lifetime taxes overall.

From a Social Security perspective, the key advantage is straightforward: by shrinking your traditional IRA or 401(k) balances before you claim benefits — or before RMDs become substantial —

you reduce the future impact those accounts have on provisional income. That means fewer years where 85% of your Social Security is taxable, and fewer years where an extra withdrawal pushes you into a punishingly high marginal rate purely because it triggers more Social Security taxation alongside it.

When to Consider Roth Conversions

Timing is everything with Roth conversions. Convert during a very high-income year, or after RMDs are already substantial, and you may simply compound the tax problem rather than solve it. The genuinely best windows tend to be:

- The years between retirement and the start of Social Security.
- The years between claiming one spouse's benefit and claiming the other's.
- The years between retirement and the beginning of RMDs.

During these windows, your income may genuinely be lower than it will be later, especially if you design your withdrawals carefully around it. You can convert just enough each year to "fill up" a lower tax bracket without spilling over into a much higher one. Doing this gradually — converting a manageable amount each year throughout your 60s, say — can meaningfully shrink your future RMDs and their downstream impact on provisional income.

Age and health are another timing consideration worth weighing. If one spouse has a significantly higher life expectancy, or is likely to outlive the other by many years, reducing future RMDs becomes especially valuable. After one spouse dies, the survivor typically files as single — meaning lower standard deductions, tighter tax brackets, and noticeably lower Social Security tax thresholds, exactly as covered earlier in this chapter. A Roth-heavy balance sheet can genuinely soften that tax burden for whichever spouse ends up surviving.

You'll also want to coordinate conversions with the other life events covered throughout this book: when you plan to downsize, when you might sell a business, when pensions start, or when you intend to make large charitable gifts. Any event that spikes your income in a particular year makes that year a poor candidate for a conversion, while years with minimal extra income are prime opportunities you don't want to waste.

Balancing Immediate Tax Costs vs. Long-Term Savings

Roth conversions aren't automatically beneficial — the advantage depends entirely on the relationship between the tax rate you pay today and the tax rate you'd otherwise pay on those same withdrawals later. If you're already in a high bracket now, and genuinely expect to be in a much lower bracket in retirement, conversion may not be attractive at all.

From a Social Security tax perspective, though, you have to look beyond the headline bracket numbers. Consider the marginal tax effect when extra traditional withdrawals simultaneously raise your taxable income and increase the share of your Social Security that's taxed. In certain income ranges, that combined effect can push your effective marginal rate well above your stated bracket — sometimes dramatically so. Conversions done earlier, in years when you're not yet receiving Social Security, or before you've reached the 85% threshold, can prevent you from getting caught in that high marginal zone year after year, later on, when you have far less flexibility to avoid it.

Still, it's entirely possible to over-convert. Move too much money in a single year and you may push your current-year income into much higher tax brackets, or trigger side effects like increased Medicare premiums or the loss of valuable tax credits. In that case, you could end up paying more in taxes right now than you save later — the opposite of the intended effect. This is exactly why careful projections matter so much here. Model several scenarios — no conversions, modest annual conversions, more aggressive conversions — and compare lifetime taxes under each before committing to a path.

The guiding principle is moderation paired with genuine awareness. Convert enough to meaningfully reduce future RMDs and Social Security taxation, but not so much that you create a significant short-term tax problem in the process. It's almost always better to convert steadily over several years than to attempt one dramatic, one-time shift.

Other Planning Tools: Charitable Giving and Annuities

Roth strategies aren't the only way to manage Social Security taxation. Two other tools — qualified charitable distributions (QCDs) and certain types of annuities — can also play a meaningful role.

Qualified charitable distributions let IRA owners above a certain age direct money from their IRA straight to a qualified charity. The distribution counts toward your RMD for the year, but it's not included in your taxable income at all. Because it never passes through your adjusted gross income, it also never increases your provisional income. This can be a genuinely tax-efficient way for charitably inclined retirees to support causes they care about, while simultaneously keeping more of their Social Security sheltered from tax.

For example, if you're required to take a $20,000 RMD and you planned to give $5,000 to charity anyway, you can arrange a $5,000 QCD and withdraw only the remaining $15,000 for yourself. Your AGI is based on that $15,000, not the full $20,000, which may help keep you below a provisional income threshold, or reduce the percentage of your Social Security that's taxable. You don't get a separate charitable deduction for the QCD itself, but you've effectively made your charitable giving "pre-tax" in a way a regular donation never could.

Annuities are more complex, and their tax treatment varies depending on whether they're held in taxable accounts or IRAs, plus the specific type of annuity involved. In general, income from annuities that flows into your AGI will affect provisional income and Social Security taxation just like any other income source. But certain annuity designs can spread taxable income more evenly across time, helping you avoid the sharp spikes that push you into the 85% zone in particular years.

In some retirement income plans — particularly those designed around sequence-of-returns risk and guaranteed income, which we'll cover in later chapters — an annuity gets used specifically to cover essential expenses. If that annuity replaces the need for large, irregular IRA withdrawals, it can lead to a more predictable, manageable provisional income pattern over time, even if it doesn't directly reduce the percentage of Social Security that's taxable on its own.

As with any specialized financial product, it's important to understand the fees, surrender charges, and trade-offs before committing to an annuity. Its value for Social Security tax planning is typically a secondary benefit, not the primary reason to buy one in the first place.

Charitable tools and annuities both illustrate a broader point that connects this entire chapter back to the rest of the book: tax planning for Social Security can't be separated from your other goals. Giving, guaranteed income, leaving a legacy for children, and protecting a surviving spouse all intersect, in one way or another, with the question of how much of your Social Security you actually get to keep. As you move into later chapters on comprehensive retirement planning, hold onto the concept of provisional income. Whenever someone proposes a new investment, a withdrawal strategy, or an insurance product, one of your very first questions should be: "How will this affect my Social Security taxation, both now and later?"

By understanding the rules and actively using the tools available — timed withdrawals, Roth accounts, well-placed conversions, intentional use of low-income years, QCDs, and potentially annuities — you can turn Social Security from a confusing tax puzzle into a stable, efficient foundation for your retirement. Even small improvements in how much of your benefit you keep, repeated year after year, can make a genuinely meaningful difference in the comfort and freedom you experience throughout the decades after you stop working.

The Bottom Line

Your Social Security check isn't automatically tax-free, and it isn't automatically 85% taxable either — it depends entirely on your provisional income, a number built from your other income plus tax-exempt interest plus half your benefit. The thresholds that decide your fate haven't moved since the 1990s, which means more retirees get pulled into taxation every year without changing their behavior at all. The good news: you have real levers — withdrawal timing, Roth conversions, QCDs, and where you hold which investments — to manage where you land.

KEY TAKEAWAYS

• Provisional income — your AGI plus tax-exempt interest plus half your Social Security benefit — determines whether 0%, up to 50%, or up to 85% of your benefit is taxable.

• The thresholds ($25,000/$34,000 single; $32,000/$44,000 married) haven't been adjusted for inflation since the 1980s and 1990s, which quietly pulls more retirees into taxation every year.

• Once you're in the phase-in zone, extra income can trigger a hidden marginal rate increase — an extra $1,000 IRA withdrawal can functionally cost you tax on $1,850, not $1,000.

• Roth withdrawals never count toward provisional income. Building Roth balances before retirement, or converting strategically during low-income years, is one of the most powerful tools available for controlling future Social Security taxation.

• Qualified charitable distributions let you satisfy your RMD and support causes you care about without that money ever touching your AGI — a genuine double benefit for anyone who gives regularly.

Next up: what actually happens to your benefit if you keep working — the earnings test explained properly, why withheld benefits usually aren't gone forever, and how to coordinate part-time income with your claiming strategy.

Chapter 7: Work, Part-Time Income, and Benefits: What Continuing to Earn Means

Chapter at a Glance

What you'll learn in this chapter:

• How the earnings test actually works — and why withheld benefits are usually deferred, not lost

• The specific dollar formula behind the "$1 for every $2" rule, and the more generous version that applies the year you reach FRA

• How to report your earnings correctly and avoid an unexpected overpayment notice

• How to coordinate part-time work with your claiming age to build a strategy that fits your actual life

Estimated reading time: 25 minutes

> ***FIELD NOTE*** *A client once told me her coworker swore that going back to work after claiming Social Security meant she'd "lose her benefits forever." That coworker was wrong, but I understand exactly why she believed it — the rule genuinely does withhold checks in the short term, and nobody explains the part where you mostly get it back. This chapter is that explanation.*

Retirement today rarely resembles a clean break between "working" and "not working." For a lot of people, it's closer to a dimmer switch than an on/off button. You might scale down your hours, take on consulting projects, or pick up a part-time role that keeps you engaged and brings in some extra income on the side. But the moment you start picturing that paycheck alongside your Social Security benefit, an important question shows up: how exactly do the two interact?

You've probably heard warnings that working "too much" while collecting Social Security can make you "lose" benefits. Maybe a coworker insists you should never claim early if you plan to keep working, or a friend tells you their check "disappeared" for several months because of their earnings. Underneath these stories sits a real set of rules — but the way people describe them is usually wrong, or at least missing the second half of the story. The reality is more nuanced, and often considerably more favorable, than the rumors suggest.

This chapter exists to turn that confusion into clarity. We'll unpack the earnings test, explain exactly what happens once your income crosses certain thresholds, and show you why withheld benefits generally aren't gone forever — they come back. We'll also look at how your ongoing work history can actually increase your benefit over time, how to report income correctly to avoid unpleasant surprises, and how to coordinate part-time earnings with your claiming age to build a genuinely thoughtful, personalized income plan.

Earlier in this book, you learned the basics of how Social Security calculates your benefit and how different claiming ages change your monthly check. Now we're layering work income into that same picture. Think of this chapter as the bridge between the "when to claim" questions from earlier chapters and the broader retirement income planning you'll tackle later, where taxes, investments, and long-term security all come together. By the end, you should feel equipped not just to answer "Can I keep working?" but the more useful question: "How should I work, and when should I claim, to support the retirement life I actually want?"

7.1 Understanding the Earnings Test: Temporary and Permanent Effects

The first concept to master is the earnings test, formally called the Retirement Earnings Test. It's the rule that determines how your wages or self-employment income can affect your Social Security checks before you reach your full retirement age. FRA is the age — typically between 66 and 67, depending on your birth year — when you can receive your full, unreduced retirement benefit. Once you reach FRA, the earnings test disappears completely. Before that point, it can matter quite a lot.

The earnings test isn't a tax, and it isn't a permanent penalty either. It's a timing rule. It controls when you receive some of your benefits, not whether you receive them at all. Still, because it touches your cash flow in the near term, it can feel like a genuine penalty if you weren't expecting it. Understanding exactly how it works — both in the years before FRA and in the specific months when you reach it — can change your planning decisions considerably.

How the Earnings Test Works Before Full Retirement Age

If you start your Social Security retirement or survivor benefits before reaching FRA and continue working, the earnings test applies. Each calendar year, there's an annual earnings limit for anyone who hasn't yet reached FRA. Stay below that limit and your Social Security checks are paid in full. Earn more than the limit, and Social Security withholds part of your benefit.

The formula is straightforward: for every \$2 you earn above the annual limit, Social Security withholds \$1 in benefits for that year. The exact limit changes periodically, but the structure stays the same year after year.

Imagine you're 63, already receiving retirement benefits, and expecting some part-time wages. Suppose the annual limit for that year works out to \$25,000 (check ssa.gov for the actual current-year figure, since it changes annually). Earn \$25,000 or less and the earnings test never touches your benefits. Earn \$30,000 instead, and you're \$5,000 above the limit. Social Security would withhold \$2,500 in benefits for that year — \$1 for every \$2 of excess earnings.

People often assume those withheld dollars are simply gone. They're not. Social Security keeps track of exactly which months your benefits were fully or partially withheld, and uses those months later to adjust your benefit upward once you reach full retirement age. In the meantime, though, you genuinely do have less cash arriving in your bank account, which is exactly why planning around the test matters in the short term. The key is weighing the value of that paycheck —

even with some withholding attached — against the alternative of not working, or not claiming benefits yet at all.

Another common worry is that working a lower-paying job might somehow drag down your eventual Social Security benefit. That's a completely separate question from the earnings test, and it loops back to how your benefit gets calculated in the first place — based on your highest 35 years of inflation-adjusted earnings, as covered in Chapter 1. A few years of part-time income won't pull your benefit down unless they replace higher-earning years among your top 35, which is uncommon late in a career. For a lot of people, late-career or post-retirement earnings actually exceed some early-career years, or replace literal zero years — so working, even part-time, can genuinely raise your future benefit rather than reduce it.

The Year You Reach Full Retirement Age

The rules change in the specific calendar year you reach your full retirement age. A lot of people assume the same "$1 for every $2" rule applies right up until their birthday. Instead, the Social Security Administration uses a noticeably more generous test for this "bridge" year.

In the year you reach FRA, the annual earnings limit is higher, and the withholding formula is less strict. For the months before your birthday month, Social Security withholds $1 in benefits for every $3 you earn above that higher limit. They only count earnings from January up to the month before you reach FRA — earnings in or after the month you actually reach FRA are ignored entirely for this particular test.

Consider an example. Suppose you reach your FRA in August. Your monthly benefit at that time is $800. That year, the special higher limit for people reaching FRA might be, say, $65,000 (again, check ssa.gov for the current figure). Earn $66,000 in wages across the first seven months of the year and you're $1,000 over the limit. Social Security takes $1 in benefits for every $3 above that limit, so they'd withhold a total of $333. On a yearly basis, you were due $5,600 for January through July — seven months of $800 — but you actually receive $5,320 because of that $333 withholding. Starting in August, when you reach FRA, you receive your full $800 a month regardless of how much you earn from that point forward.

Notice how different this looks from the stricter rule that applies before your FRA year. You were over the limit, yet only a small portion of your benefits got withheld, and only for the months before your FRA month specifically. This is exactly why planning around the year you reach FRA can give you genuine flexibility: if you want to ramp up your hours, or accept a higher-paying role knowing you're close to FRA, the actual impact is usually smaller than people fear going in.

No Earnings Test After Full Retirement Age

Once you reach your full retirement age, the earnings test no longer applies at all. From that month onward, you can work and earn as much as you like — part-time, full-time, or beyond — without any reduction whatsoever to your Social Security benefit.

At that stage, your decision to keep working becomes driven entirely by your goals, your energy, and the opportunities in front of you — not by any fear of losing benefits. You might continue in your current role, shift to part-time, or chase a passion project with genuinely unpredictable income. Whatever you choose, Social Security pays your full benefit every single month. This freedom lets you think more broadly about your work and income choices, which is exactly what later chapters on integrating Social Security with tax strategy and portfolio withdrawals will help you do.

There's another upside here that loops back to Chapter 1's explanation of how your benefit gets calculated. Social Security recalculates your benefit every year to check whether your latest earnings are high enough to replace one of the lower-earning years among your top 35. You continue paying Social Security payroll taxes on your wages for as long as you work. If, at 68, you have a strong consulting year that exceeds one of your early-career years of low or zero earnings, that new year can replace a weaker year in your calculation and raise your benefit. The increase doesn't happen instantly, but the following year you'll see a higher monthly amount, retroactive to the prior January.

This possibility alone is exactly why some retirees choose to keep working, even modestly, past their FRA: the combination of ongoing income plus a slightly higher Social Security benefit can offer genuinely meaningful protection against both inflation and longevity risk over a long retirement.

Permanent Benefit Adjustments Due to Earnings Surplus

We've discussed the earnings test as a temporary withholding mechanism, not a permanent loss. So how exactly do you "get back" what was withheld? The answer lies in a recalculation Social Security performs once you reach your full retirement age.

When you first claim benefits before your FRA, your monthly check gets permanently reduced relative to what it would have been had you waited. That reduction is based on the number of months between your claiming date and your FRA. Suppose your FRA is 67, but you claimed at 62 — that's 60 months early. Now imagine that between ages 62 and 67, you worked enough that the earnings test caused Social Security to withhold a total of 18 months' worth of your benefit. At your FRA, they adjust your benefit as if you had only claimed 42 months early instead of 60. In other words, they erase the early-claiming reduction for the months in which you effectively didn't receive benefits, because they were withheld.

That adjustment results in a higher monthly benefit going forward, for the rest of your life. You don't get a lump-sum repayment for what was withheld — instead, you get a larger check every month, permanently, than you would have otherwise received. Over a long retirement, this can fully offset the earlier withholding, and the longer you live, the more that adjustment works in your favor.

The catch is purely about timing. While you're under your FRA, the earnings test can create real cash-flow pressure in the moment. Bills still need to be paid even if your Social Security check is partially or fully withheld for part of the year. If you rely heavily on those benefits for everyday expenses, unexpected withholding can feel like a genuine financial shock when it happens. This is exactly why it's worth connecting what we're covering here to the overall claiming strategies and budgeting guidance from earlier chapters. The more clearly you anticipate your work income, and understand how it interacts with the earnings test, the easier it becomes to choose a claiming age that genuinely fits your needs.

In short: working while you receive benefits doesn't permanently harm you under the earnings test rules. It can even help you, by raising your benefit calculation and crediting you for the months your benefit was withheld. The interim impact on cash flow is real, though – and that's exactly what the next section helps you manage.

7.2 Reporting Earnings & Navigating Recoupment Rules

Knowing the rules conceptually is only half the battle. To make them genuinely work in your favor, you need to understand how earnings get reported to Social Security, how overpayments happen, and what to do if the agency decides you were paid more than you should have been. Clean reporting and a bit of proactive planning can save you real headaches and unpleasant surprises down the line.

How Earnings Are Reported to Social Security

For most people, earnings reach Social Security through familiar channels. If you're an employee, your employer reports your wages to the SSA as part of the standard payroll tax process. When your employer withholds Social Security and Medicare taxes from your paycheck, they're simultaneously filing forms that show your total wages for the year. These records eventually become part of your Social Security earnings history.

If you're self-employed, the process works a little differently. Instead of an employer reporting wages on your behalf, you report your own net earnings from self-employment on your tax return, using Schedule SE. After you file your federal income tax return, the IRS sends that earnings information to Social Security, and your self-employment earnings get added to your record. "Net earnings" means your gross business income minus allowable business expenses, so accurate bookkeeping genuinely matters here.

Because the agency relies so heavily on these tax and payroll reports, errors can and do occur. A missing W-2, a name mismatch, or a typo in a Social Security number can cause your earnings to be under-recorded or misapplied somewhere along the line. To guard against this, review your Social Security earnings record periodically — by creating and monitoring an online account, or by reviewing the statements Social Security mails or makes available electronically. Spot missing or incorrect earnings, and you can work with your employer or the agency directly to get them corrected.

Some income sources don't count as "earnings" for purposes of the retirement earnings test at all. Investment income, pensions, annuities, IRA or 401(k) withdrawals, rental income, and government benefits like veterans' compensation don't factor into the earnings test calculation. Wages, bonuses, commissions, and net self-employment income are the primary forms of income that actually matter for this specific rule — worth knowing if you're trying to estimate whether you'll cross the limit in a given year.

Keeping pay stubs, year-end W-2 forms, 1099s, and tax returns organized pays off the moment any question arises. If Social Security sends you a letter about your earnings or your benefits, having those records on hand makes it considerably easier to respond quickly and accurately, rather than scrambling to reconstruct your income history under time pressure.

Overpayments and Recoupment Explained

Even when everyone is acting in complete good faith, the interplay between expected earnings, actual earnings, and benefit payments can get out of sync. Maybe you told Social Security you planned to earn $20,000 this year, but then a part-time role expanded, or you picked up an unexpected consulting contract, and your wages ended up rising above the earnings limit. If Social Security kept paying full benefits based on your earlier estimate, you may end up having received more than the rules actually allow for that year. That excess is called an overpayment.

When an overpayment occurs, Social Security notifies you by letter. The notice explains why they believe an overpayment happened, how much they think you owe, and how they plan to recover it. The most common recoupment method is withholding future benefits until the overpayment is fully repaid. If they determine you were overpaid by $3,000, for example, they might withhold your entire check for several months, or withhold a smaller portion of each check over a longer stretch of time instead.

From Social Security's perspective, this is simply correcting the earnings test after the fact. From your perspective, it can feel like a sudden, unwelcome cut to your income — especially if you've been relying on those benefits to cover everyday expenses. That's exactly why understanding how the test works, and monitoring your earnings closely throughout the year, matters so much. Preventing overpayments is almost always considerably easier than dealing with recoupment after the fact.

It also helps to realize that Social Security's process isn't instantaneous. Earnings data from employers and the IRS arrives only after the year ends. In some cases, overpayments get discovered a year or more after the fact — long after the money has already been spent. This delay is another good reason to build a margin of safety into your plans if you're working and claiming benefits before your full retirement age.

What to Do If You Disagree with Recoupment

Sometimes the overpayment notice is simply incorrect, or at least incomplete. The agency might have misclassified certain income, overlooked business expenses that reduce your self-employment earnings, or misunderstood your actual work pattern. If you receive a letter that doesn't match your own understanding of your earnings or benefits, you're not powerless here.

You have the right to request a reconsideration, or file an appeal, within the timeframe specified on the notice. To make that request effective, gather documentation: W-2 forms, 1099s, pay stubs, tax returns, and any correspondence you previously sent to Social Security about your expected earnings. Clear, organized records make it considerably easier to demonstrate exactly how much you actually earned, and when.

If you agree an overpayment occurred but genuinely can't afford the proposed repayment schedule, you can often negotiate a different arrangement. Social Security may allow smaller withholdings spread across more months, or, in certain hardship situations, they may waive part or all of an overpayment entirely. The specifics depend on your circumstances and the details of your case, so it can be worth seeking guidance from a Social Security expert, a financial planner familiar with the system, or, in some cases, an attorney who specializes in benefits.

The key point: you're not obligated to accept the initial notice without question. The process can feel bureaucratic, but the rules do allow for corrections, and for genuine consideration of your ability to repay.

Avoiding Overpayments by Planning Earnings

The simplest way to minimize overpayment headaches is to plan your earnings carefully and keep Social Security informed of significant changes as they happen. Before you claim benefits while still working, sit down and estimate your likely yearly wages or self-employment income. This is where your broader retirement planning comes into play — earlier chapters encouraged you to think through your spending needs and desired lifestyle; now add your work plans into that picture and translate them into expected income for the year.

If you're close to the earnings limit for a given year, small adjustments can genuinely make a difference. You might negotiate your hours or schedule to stay under the threshold. You might delay a bonus, or postpone a consulting project until the following calendar year — especially if you'll reach your FRA that later year and face the considerably more generous earnings test, or no test at all.

Once you've started receiving benefits, keep an eye on your actual earnings as the year unfolds. If your income turns out higher or lower than planned, inform Social Security promptly. Reporting changes by phone or in person at a local office lets the agency adjust your benefit withholding during the year, rather than discovering a large discrepancy after the fact. This reduces your odds of receiving a painful overpayment notice, and smooths out your monthly cash flow considerably.

Finally, review your Social Security statements and earnings history regularly. Spotting errors early — a missing year of earnings, for instance — gives you time to correct the record before it affects your benefits, or triggers an unexpected interaction with the earnings test down the line. Treat your Social Security record as a critical financial document, worth checking just as seriously as your bank statements or investment accounts.

By managing your work income with the earnings test in mind, and staying in communication with Social Security as things change, you turn the system from something that "happens to you" into a tool you navigate deliberately, on your own terms.

7.3 Coordinating Part-Time Work with Benefit Timing

Now that you understand how the earnings test works and how to report earnings correctly, the final piece is strategy. How do you actually combine part-time work and your Social Security claiming decision to support your broader retirement goals? There's no single right answer here — the best approach depends on your health, your longevity expectations, your financial resources, your family situation, and the nature of the work itself. Still, there are clear patterns worth understanding as you think through your own trade-offs.

This is exactly where the concepts from earlier chapters — the impact of claiming early versus delaying, and the importance of longevity risk — connect directly to your work life. In later chapters, we'll layer in taxes and other income sources on top of these choices, but for now, we're focused purely on the direct interaction between work and benefit timing.

Delaying Benefits to Boost Monthly Payments

One genuinely powerful strategy for anyone planning to keep working, even part-time, is delaying your Social Security claim. If your job income covers your essential expenses, you may not need your Social Security check right away. By postponing your claim past your full retirement age, you earn delayed retirement credits that increase your monthly benefit all the way up to age 70.

These credits add a significant percentage to your check for every year you delay past FRA. Over a long retirement, the cumulative effect of a permanently higher monthly benefit can be substantial. The income you earn from working during this period essentially becomes a bridge that lets you postpone tapping into Social Security at all. Meanwhile, your continued earnings may further raise your eventual benefit, by replacing lower-earning years in your lifetime record — exactly the mechanism covered in Chapter 1.

This approach is particularly attractive for people in good health who expect to live into their eighties or beyond. The trade-off is straightforward: fewer years of receiving benefits, in exchange for larger checks for the rest of your life. If part-time or consulting work feels sustainable and genuinely satisfying, it can be an elegant way to fund those deferral years without sacrificing your day-to-day quality of life.

Of course, delaying isn't always ideal. If you have significant health concerns, a family history of shorter lifespans, or limited financial resources outside Social Security, claiming earlier may still be the sensible choice. The point is that having part-time income genuinely expands your menu of options. Instead of feeling forced to claim early purely because you "need the money," you may be able to choose to delay, knowing your work is filling the gap in the meantime.

Claiming Early While Working Part-Time: Pros and Cons

On the other hand, plenty of people claim Social Security before reaching their FRA while still working part-time. This is common for anyone who reduces their hours in their early sixties and wants Social Security to help replace part of their lost income. It can be a perfectly reasonable choice, but one that deserves a careful look before you commit to it.

The main advantage is simple: immediate income. Reduce your work hours, and if your employer doesn't offer phased retirement options, your paycheck may shrink considerably. Early Social Security benefits can ease that transition and give you more freedom to actually enjoy the newly available time. For someone who's tired, stressed, or facing a job they no longer enjoy, that has real value that doesn't show up cleanly in a spreadsheet.

There are three key downsides worth weighing, though. First, claiming early permanently reduces your monthly benefit, even after you reach full retirement age. The later adjustment for months when benefits were withheld due to the earnings test helps, but it doesn't completely eliminate the early-claiming reduction, unless your benefits were withheld for the entire period — which is uncommon in practice. Second, if your part-time earnings exceed the annual limit, the earnings test may cause Social Security to withhold part of your benefit. That means you could be simultaneously locking in a lower lifetime benefit while not even fully receiving the reduced checks right now.

Third, early claiming may reduce survivor benefits for a spouse who might outlive you, especially if your earnings history is higher than theirs. As covered in Chapter 4, the highest earner's claiming decisions often shape the couple's long-term security as a household. If you're that higher earner, think carefully before claiming early purely to supplement a relatively short period of part-time work.

So when might early claiming while working part-time genuinely make sense? It can be appropriate if you need immediate cash flow and lack other resources, if you're reducing your work hours permanently rather than temporarily, or if health issues make a longer life genuinely unlikely. It can also be reasonable if your earnings stay low enough that you remain below the earnings limit, avoiding withholding altogether. The key is approaching the decision with your eyes fully open, understanding the trade-offs for both you and your spouse over decades — not just for this year alone.

Creating Customized Work-Benefit Plans

No two retirements look exactly alike, and no single rule can capture the full complexity of individual situations. That's why it helps to think in terms of scenarios, rather than chasing one absolute answer. Start with a few basic questions: How long do you realistically want to keep working, and in what capacity? How important is flexibility compared to maximizing income? How's your health, and what does your family history suggest about longevity? What savings, pensions, or other income do you have beyond Social Security and work itself?

Once you've clarified these factors, sketch out a few different paths. Scenario A might involve continuing full-time work until full retirement age, then claiming benefits and cutting back to part-time. Scenario B might involve leaving full-time work at 62, picking up occasional consulting, and delaying Social Security until 67 or 70. Scenario C might involve early claiming at 62 combined with a steady, modest part-time role, staying carefully under the earnings limit the whole time.

For each scenario, you — or a financial advisor — can run simple calculations: estimate total income by year, account for the earnings test where it applies, and project your monthly Social Security benefit based on the different claiming ages involved. Interactive tools can help with some of this math, but you can get most of the way there with a spreadsheet, your Social Security statement, and a clear understanding of the rules from this chapter and the ones before it.

Scenario planning also helps you prepare for change. Maybe you intend to work part-time until 70, but find at 66 that your energy has dropped, or caregiving responsibilities have increased unexpectedly. Or maybe you expect to cut back, but discover that consulting opportunities are abundant and genuinely rewarding. Revisiting your plan every year or two, and updating it based on reality rather than your original assumptions, makes your retirement path considerably more resilient. The knowledge you're building throughout this book

— how work affects Social Security, how taxes interact with benefits, how to coordinate with investments — gives you the flexibility to pivot rather than feel boxed in by a decision you made years earlier.

Communicating with Employers and Tax Professionals

Finally, working in retirement isn't purely about your relationship with Social Security — it also involves employers, clients, and tax professionals. Clear communication with all of them makes your life considerably easier, and your overall plan more effective.

When talking with employers, it helps to discuss your desired hours, workload, and schedule well in advance. If you're trying to keep your earnings under a specific threshold to avoid the earnings test, say so directly. A lot of employers appreciate that clarity, and may be willing to adjust roles, shift bonuses or overtime timing, or design part-time structures that align with your goals. Consultants or self-employed workers might negotiate project timing so larger payments land in years when they're already past their full retirement age, and no longer subject to the earnings test at all.

Tax advisers can help you see well beyond Social Security to the broader picture. Wages and self-employment income affect not just the earnings test, but also your income tax bracket, the taxation of your Social Security benefits (covered in depth in Chapter 6), Medicare premiums, and decisions around IRA or 401(k) withdrawals. Coordinated planning may reveal opportunities to smooth income across several years, convert some savings to Roth accounts while your earnings are temporarily modest, or time capital gains for years when your work income happens to be low. These topics get explored more fully in later chapters focused on taxes and integrating income streams — but it's worth recognizing now that the choices you make about part-time work carry far-reaching implications well beyond your current paycheck.

Bringing your Social Security considerations into these conversations also improves the quality of advice you receive. When your tax preparer knows you're weighing whether to claim at 62 or 67, or when your financial planner understands your desire to keep earnings under the limit, they can tailor their guidance accordingly.

Instead of making isolated decisions about work, Social Security, taxes, and investments separately, you end up with a genuinely integrated plan that actually fits together.

Retirement is no longer a finish line you cross and leave behind — it's a stage of life that may include many forms of work, multiple income sources, and several significant decisions about when and how to claim Social Security. By learning how the earnings test operates, how to report earnings accurately, and how to coordinate part-time income with your claiming strategy, you give yourself more genuine choices, and considerably fewer unpleasant surprises along the way.

The chapters that follow build on this foundation, exploring how to weave Social Security into the rest of your financial life — taxes, savings, healthcare, and legacy planning — so that whether you work a little, a lot, or not at all in retirement, your benefits support the life you've actually envisioned for yourself.

The Bottom Line

The earnings test scares people more than it should, mostly because nobody explains the second half of the rule: withheld benefits generally come back as a permanent increase once you reach full retirement age. Working while claiming early isn't a mistake — it's a trade-off between near-term cash flow and long-term benefit size, and it deserves the same deliberate decision-making as every other choice in this book. After FRA, the entire question disappears, and work becomes purely about what you want, not what Social Security allows.

KEY TAKEAWAYS

• The earnings test only applies before your full retirement age. Earn above the annual limit and Social Security withholds $1 for every $2 over it — but those withheld months get credited back as a permanent benefit increase once you reach FRA.

• The year you actually reach FRA uses a far more generous test: a higher earnings limit, and only $1 withheld for every $3 over it, counting only the months before your birthday month.

• After FRA, there is no earnings test at all. Work as much as you want without any reduction to your Social Security benefit — and continued strong earnings can still raise your benefit by replacing a weaker year in your top 35.

• Overpayments happen when actual earnings exceed what you estimated. Reporting income changes promptly, and keeping organized records (W-2s, 1099s, pay stubs), is the easiest way to avoid a painful surprise notice later.

• There's no universal right answer between claiming early while working part-time and delaying to let work bridge the gap. The right choice depends on your immediate cash needs, your health outlook, and — if you're married — what your claiming decision means for your spouse's eventual survivor benefit.

Next up: the special cases that change the playbook entirely — government pensions, the now-repealed WEP and GPO provisions, disability transitions, military service, and railroad retirement, and why your story might not match the standard rules covered so far.

Chapter 8: Special Cases & Exceptions: Rules That Change the Playbook

Chapter at a Glance

What you'll learn in this chapter:

• What the Windfall Elimination Provision and Government Pension Offset actually were — and why their 2025 repeal matters for anyone who received older estimates

• How to tell whether your career crossed into "non-covered" employment, and why that question used to change everything

• How disability benefits transition seamlessly into retirement benefits at full retirement age

• The special rules surrounding divorce, military service, railroad retirement, and federal employment that don't fit the standard playbook

Estimated reading time: 24 minutes

> ***FIELD NOTE*** *I had a client — a retired teacher — who showed up with a benefit estimate from 2019 that was nearly half what a private-sector worker with the same earnings history would have received. She thought something was wrong with her record. Nothing was wrong. She'd simply been caught by a provision called WEP, which most people in fully-covered careers never even hear about. That provision is gone now. But if you ever received an estimate like hers, you need to know it doesn't apply anymore.*

For most people, Social Security feels like a straightforward path: you work, you pay in, you claim, you receive a check. But if you've spent part of your career in government, teaching, law enforcement, the military, overseas, or inside a separate pension system, that straight path suddenly bends in ways the standard chapters in this book don't fully cover. Special provisions like the Windfall Elimination Provision (WEP) and the Government Pension Offset (GPO) were designed to address these unusual circumstances, and for decades they reduced benefits for a lot of public servants and their families. However, the Social Security Fairness Act, signed on January 5, 2025, repealed both provisions for benefits payable for January 2024 and later.

At first glance, rules like these can feel like traps. You might hear someone say, "I thought my benefit would be X, but when I filed, it was Y — and nobody warned me." Or, "We were counting on a spousal benefit, but then we learned about the GPO and lost most of it." These aren't fringe stories. They were common, lived experiences for teachers, firefighters, police officers, city and state employees, and anyone with "non-covered" work where no Social Security tax was withheld.

This chapter is about those twists in the playbook. Because WEP and GPO were repealed by the Social Security Fairness Act, this chapter should now be read primarily as historical context, and as background for anyone reviewing older benefit estimates, prior planning advice, or legacy pension discussions. We'll explain what WEP and GPO actually were, why they existed, and how public pensions, survivor planning, disability, divorce, military and railroad systems, and other special cases can still affect retirement decisions even after the repeal.

By the end, you should be able to look at your own work history — or a client's — and say: "Here's whether older estimates or prior advice were affected by WEP or GPO, here's what changed after their repeal, here's how transitions like disability or divorce could still alter the picture, and here's the planning conversation we need to have now." Whether you're an individual nearing retirement, a couple trying to coordinate pensions and Social Security, or an advisor guiding others through complex choices, understanding these exceptions matters for avoiding surprises and maximizing lifetime income.

8.1 Government Pensions and the Windfall Elimination Provision (WEP)

For decades, the Windfall Elimination Provision was one of the most misunderstood corners of the entire Social Security system. It didn't apply to most workers, which is exactly why a lot of people never heard of it at all. But for a specific subset of retirees — particularly public sector employees with pensions from non-covered work — it could reduce monthly benefits by hundreds of dollars. The provision was repealed by the Social Security Fairness Act, so this section now serves as historical background rather than current-law planning guidance.

What Was the Windfall Elimination Provision (WEP)?

WEP was a special rule triggered when three ingredients were present at once: a government or other "non-covered" pension, some Social Security-covered work, and eligibility for a Social Security retirement or disability benefit based on that covered work. It no longer applies to benefits payable for January 2024 and later, since it was repealed by the Social Security Fairness Act. "Non-covered" meant the employer hadn't withheld Social Security taxes — common for certain state and local government jobs, teachers in some systems, public safety workers like police officers and firefighters, and some foreign employers.

As you saw in Chapter 1, Social Security's basic benefit formula is progressive — it replaces a higher percentage of low lifetime earnings than high earnings. If your Social Security record showed only a small amount of covered work, because much of your career sat inside a non-covered government job, the system treated you as a lifetime low-wage worker — even if you were also collecting a generous government pension on the side. Lawmakers viewed this as a "windfall" relative to other Social Security workers with similar total earnings but no separate pension. WEP was created specifically to address that perceived double advantage.

In practice, if you spent part of your career in a public job that didn't pay into Social Security, and you earned a pension from that work, your own Social Security worker benefit could be reduced. WEP never touched benefits other people received based on your record — a spouse's spousal benefit, or your children's benefits — it only changed your own retirement or disability benefit. And it never affected your government pension itself; your pension was calculated entirely under your employer's own rules. WEP only changed how Social Security viewed your Social Security-covered earnings, nothing else.

Figuring out whether you have a "non-covered" pension is step one in understanding whether WEP ever applied to you historically. A lot of people with a CalPERS teacher pension, a police or fire pension, or a state university pension fall into this category. So do some workers with foreign pensions earned in jobs where no U.S. Social Security tax was paid. If you have a pension like this, plus some years of Social Security-covered work in other jobs, WEP was part of your story — at least until the repeal.

How WEP Reduced Benefits: The Formula Change

To see how WEP worked, it helps to revisit the basic Social Security formula from Chapter 1. The system computes your AIME from your highest 35 years of inflation-adjusted wages subject to Social Security tax, then applies a three-part formula with "bend points" where the replacement percentage changes. Before WEP, the formula looked roughly like this (the dollar amounts adjust each year, but the structure stays the same):

1. 90% of your AIME up to the first bend point.
2. 32% of your AIME between the first and second bend points.
3. 15% of your AIME above the second bend point.

The key detail: the first slice of your earnings gets a much higher replacement rate — 90% — which is exactly why low-earning workers receive a relatively high benefit compared to their wages, by design.

Under WEP, the government didn't change your AIME or your earnings history at all. Instead, it altered the replacement rate on that first slice specifically. Rather than 90%, WEP could reduce that factor to as low as 40%, depending on how many years of "substantial" Social Security-covered earnings you had. The fewer such years, the bigger the cut. Twenty or fewer years of substantial covered earnings, and the first bend-point factor dropped all the way to 40%. Between 21 and 29 years, the factor climbed back up in 5-point steps — for example, it would land at 65% with 25 years of substantial earnings. Once you had 30 or more years of substantial earnings, WEP stopped reducing that 90% factor entirely.

This formula change could materially lower your PIA — the benefit you'd receive at full retirement age. Because the biggest reduction landed on the portion of your earnings that normally received the most generous treatment, the impact felt disproportionate: you could see a reduction of several hundred dollars a month, even with a perfectly accurate earnings record.

There was an important safeguard built in, known as the WEP guarantee. The reduction to your Social Security benefit could never exceed one-half of the amount of your non-covered pension. That rule capped the damage in cases where the formula change would otherwise have cut your benefit by more than half.

Before the repeal, simply taking a Social Security estimate at face value could genuinely mislead you if a future non-covered pension was involved. That historical caution mattered, because older estimates and older planning advice may not have reflected the eventual WEP reduction at all. Under current law, though, WEP no longer applies to benefits payable for January 2024 and later — full stop.

Examples to Illustrate WEP Effects

Examples bring the abstract formula to life, and show exactly how years of covered employment mattered. Consider Alice. She spent a significant portion of her career in a state government job that didn't participate in Social Security, and earned a pension from that work. She also worked 20 years in the private sector in Social Security-covered jobs, with average indexed earnings around $40,000.

Without WEP, the standard formula might have produced a PIA translating to roughly $1,200 a month at her full retirement age. But because Alice had a non-covered pension and only 20 years of substantial covered earnings, WEP would have reduced the first bend-point factor from 90% to 40%. Roughly speaking, that could have cut her benefit to around $800 a month — a reduction of about $400 a month, or one-third of her expected benefit.

Now compare Alice with Bob. Bob had only 10 years of Social Security-covered work, plus a substantial government pension from his long career in a non-covered city job. With so few covered years, WEP would have hit him with the full force of the 40% factor, and given the size of his pension, the WEP guarantee might still have allowed a significant reduction. His Social Security benefit, which might otherwise have been modest but meaningful, could have shrunk dramatically — possibly by an amount close to half of the monthly pension he earned from his city job.

Both stories highlight the same lesson: WEP's impact depended heavily on how many years of substantial covered earnings someone had. Two people with similar pensions, but different histories of Social Security-covered work, could have experienced very different outcomes under the old rule.

Because this was genuinely confusing, the Social Security Administration made special WEP calculators available, so affected workers could input their own information and receive an estimate reflecting WEP's formula and the guarantee cap. For anyone trying to coordinate pensions, savings, and Social Security under the old rules, using those tools — or working with a professional who understood them — was essential whenever WEP applied.

How WEP Matters Now

Because WEP has been repealed, you generally don't need to plan around it for benefits payable for January 2024 and later. Its main relevance today is historical. If you received older advice, reviewed an older estimate, or were previously affected by WEP, you may need to revisit those numbers in light of the Social Security Fairness Act — your real benefit may now be considerably higher than what you were once told to expect.

The practical planning lesson has shifted from "how do I reduce WEP?" to "were my earlier projections or assumptions built around a rule that no longer applies?" That question matters especially for workers with public pensions, mixed covered and non-covered work histories, or prior estimates prepared before the law changed in 2025.

8.2 The Government Pension Offset (GPO) and Non-Covered Work

If WEP targeted your own worker benefit, the Government Pension Offset targeted the benefits you could receive on someone else's earning record — your spouse's. That distinction matters enormously for couples and survivors, since spousal and survivor benefits can represent a large share of total household income in retirement.

What Was the Government Pension Offset (GPO)?

The GPO reduced Social Security spousal and survivor benefits when the spouse or survivor received a pension from non-covered government work. It was repealed by the Social Security Fairness Act, and no longer applies to benefits payable for January 2024 and later. The logic mirrored WEP: lawmakers didn't want someone collecting a government pension based on their own earnings, in addition to a full Social Security benefit as a spouse or widow(er) — a benefit type designed to support people with little or no work history of their own.

Under the GPO, if you had a pension from non-covered government work and were also entitled to a spousal or survivor benefit based on your husband's, wife's, or ex-spouse's earnings record, Social Security would reduce that benefit by two-thirds of the amount of your non-covered pension. That "two-thirds rule" was the heart of the entire provision.

For example, suppose your spouse had a strong Social Security record. Without the GPO, you might have expected a spousal benefit equal to up to 50% of your spouse's full retirement age benefit, or a survivor benefit equal to as much as 100% of what your spouse received. With the GPO in the mix, you had to subtract two-thirds of your government pension from that amount — and in a lot of cases, the result landed at zero.

Unlike WEP, which applied to your own retirement or disability benefit from Social Security, the GPO only ever affected the benefits you could receive as a spouse or survivor. Your own worker benefit — if you had one based on Social Security-covered work — was never reduced by the GPO. But for a lot of government retirees with limited covered earnings, those spousal and survivor benefits were precisely what they were counting on. That's exactly why the GPO so often came as such an unpleasant surprise.

How GPO Could Significantly Cut Spousal and Survivor Benefits

Consider a simple illustration. Imagine Maria, who spent her career in a non-covered state job and receives a $900 monthly pension from that work. Her husband, John, worked entirely in Social Security-covered employment and has a full retirement age benefit of $2,000 a month.

Without the GPO, Maria might have expected a spousal benefit of up to $1,000 a month — 50% of John's $2,000 — if she claimed at her own full retirement age. With the GPO, Social Security would have calculated two-thirds of Maria's $900 pension — $600 — and subtracted that from her $1,000 spousal benefit. The result: a net spousal benefit of just $400 a month.

In a lot of cases, the numbers were even less favorable. Had Maria's pension been $1,500 a month, two-thirds of that would have been $1,000 — completely wiping out her $1,000 spousal benefit. On the survivor side, suppose John dies, and Maria, as his widow, would otherwise be entitled to his full $2,000 monthly benefit. The GPO would still have subtracted two-thirds of her $1,500 pension — $1,000 — leaving a survivor benefit of just $1,000. Her total income would have been $2,500 ($1,500 pension plus $1,000 survivor benefit), not the $3,500 she might otherwise have expected.

For couples who didn't understand these rules ahead of time, the impact on retirement plans could be severe. Spousal and survivor benefits sit at the center of the claiming strategies covered in Chapter 4 — particularly for married couples trying to coordinate when each spouse should file. But when a non-covered government pension was in play, the standard script often simply didn't apply. In extreme cases, the spousal or survivor benefit could be reduced all the way to zero, rendering many of the commonly discussed timing tactics completely irrelevant.

This is exactly why awareness of the GPO mattered so much for teachers, public safety workers, and other state and local government employees whose employment systems didn't participate in Social Security. Today, its main importance is historical — it helps explain older benefit estimates, prior planning advice, and why some retirees saw different results before the repeal. For many of these workers, others in their social circles experienced the normal Social Security spousal and survivor rules, which made it easy to assume the same patterns would apply to everyone. The GPO was the fine print that quietly changed the entire story.

Historical Exceptions and Legacy Questions Related to GPO

Before repeal, the GPO included exceptions and nuances that could make a meaningful difference. Today, those details matter mainly when reviewing older benefit determinations, prior advice, or legacy pension situations. Some government roles and pension systems were effectively exempt, because the employees paid into Social Security throughout the relevant periods. For example, a lot of federal employees hired after 1983 under the Federal Employees Retirement System (FERS) paid Social Security taxes as part of their compensation. Their pensions were considered "covered" for Social Security purposes, so GPO never reduced their spousal or survivor benefits in the first place.

There were also special provisions for certain survivors and caregivers. In some circumstances, a spouse caring for a minor or disabled child could receive a "child-in-care" spousal benefit that wasn't subject to the usual GPO reduction. The details were technical, and often required direct consultation with the Social Security Administration — but the existence of these exceptions underscores an important point: you couldn't safely assume GPO applied, or didn't apply, without understanding the precise nature of the pension and the specific benefit being claimed.

Your employment history could also matter in unexpected ways. If you had a period of non-covered government work, followed by service for the same employer under a Social Security-covered arrangement, your eventual pension might have been partially exempt from GPO, or calculated in a way that changed how GPO applied. Each pension system — whether state-wide like CalPERS, or local to a city or county — has its own rules for how benefits get earned and credited, which in turn influenced Social Security's treatment.

This is one of those areas where, as a planner or an informed retiree, it pays to adopt the mindset of a detective. Ask: Was Social Security tax withheld on this job? For which years specifically? How is the pension calculated? Does any part of the pension come from Social Security-covered work? What type of spousal or survivor benefit are we even discussing — standard, child-in-care, or divorced spouse? Then, rather than relying on generic rules, verify directly with Social Security how the GPO applied, and whether any statutory or administrative exceptions might have changed the result.

How Couples Should Revisit Older GPO-Based Planning

Now that GPO has been repealed, the key task for couples is revisiting any older planning assumptions that treated spousal or survivor benefits as reduced or unavailable because of a non-covered government pension. One powerful strategy going forward is treating the higher-earning spouse's Social Security benefit as the household's "anchor," and planning its timing carefully — exactly as covered in Chapter 4.

For example, suppose one spouse has a large government pension that was once subject to the GPO and limited Social Security earnings, while the other has a strong, fully covered Social Security record. If the GPO previously wiped out much of the government-retiree spouse's spousal benefit, the couple may have placed extra emphasis on maximizing the other spouse's worker benefit, since that drives the survivor benefit too. That might have meant delaying the higher earner's claim until 70 to lock in the largest possible check — a strategy that now pays off even more, since the GPO reduction that would once have applied to any resulting spousal benefit simply doesn't exist anymore.

Couples should also revisit work and claim timing more broadly. In some households, the non-pension spouse might have chosen to work longer specifically to build their own Social Security benefit, partly to compensate for an expected GPO-reduced spousal amount. In other households, the pension-receiving spouse might have considered part-time work in Social Security-covered employment, not to avoid GPO directly, but to build up their own Social Security worker benefit, which was never affected by GPO in the first place.

Because GPO once affected projected household income, it also had ripple effects on tax planning, housing decisions, and insurance choices. A smaller or nonexistent spousal benefit might have increased the importance of life insurance to protect a surviving spouse, or tilted a decision toward downsizing or relocating to reduce fixed expenses. These are good examples of how the exceptions covered in this chapter connect directly to other parts of this book focused on withdrawal strategies, tax management, and risk protection.

For advisors, the key now is incorporating the repeal into projections, so couples aren't still operating under outdated assumptions about income streams that no longer apply. For individuals and couples planning on their own, it's worth running the numbers fresh, and revisiting them annually. As with WEP, rules can change again, your employment or pension status can evolve, and your household needs may shift. Treat the GPO repeal not as a one-time correction, but as one of several moving pieces in a genuinely dynamic retirement plan.

8.3 Transitions and Special Rules: Disability, Early Retirement, and Other Unique Cases

Beyond WEP and GPO, several other special Social Security rules can alter benefits in ways that genuinely surprise people. These include how disability benefits transition into retirement benefits, exceptions around early retirement, and a collection of uncommon but important situations involving divorce, multiple benefit types, military service, railroad retirement, and federal employment.

Transitioning from Social Security Disability Insurance (SSDI) to Retirement Benefits

If you're receiving Social Security Disability Insurance (SSDI) and approaching full retirement age, you might wonder what happens next. Do your benefits stop? Do you need to file a new application? Will your benefit amount change?

The transition from SSDI to retirement benefits is one of the smoothest processes in the entire Social Security system. When you reach your full retirement age — exactly as defined in earlier chapters — your SSDI benefit automatically converts into a retirement benefit. You don't need to do anything. There's no new claim to file, no extra paperwork, and no interruption in payments. From your perspective, the check you receive simply continues as before, though the label in Social Security's records changes from "disability" to "retirement" behind the scenes.

In most cases, the dollar amount of your benefit stays exactly the same at the moment of conversion. That's because SSDI is essentially paying you what you would have received had you reached full retirement age and filed for retirement benefits at that point. When you actually do reach that age, the system is simply recognizing that you're now a retiree rather than a disabled worker. Cost-of-living adjustments you received while on SSDI are already baked into your payment, and continue under the retirement label without any gap.

Understanding this automatic conversion can genuinely reduce anxiety for disabled workers approaching full retirement age. Some people fear their income will drop, or that they'll need to navigate an entirely new application process. In reality, the conversion is designed to be seamless. That said, it's still wise to review your situation as you near full retirement age, especially if you're married or divorced, to see whether additional spousal or survivor benefits might become newly available once your status changes to "retired worker."

Early Retirement Exceptions and Penalty Waivers

Most people are familiar with the basic rule from Chapter 2: claiming Social Security before full retirement age reduces your monthly benefit. If your FRA is 67 and you claim at 62, you accept a permanent reduction compared to waiting. But there are exceptions and nuances that can soften — or in rare cases waive — these reductions.

Some of these exceptions relate to disability and work history. Individuals who were disabled, returned to work, and later claimed retirement benefits may accumulate special credits, or fall under provisions designed to avoid double-penalizing them. In certain narrow circumstances, the effective reduction for early retirement may be partly offset by how the system counts their years of disability, or applies particular earnings tests.

Other exceptions have arisen from legislative changes over time. When Congress has adjusted full retirement ages, or modified rules in other ways, it has sometimes created "grandfathered" categories of people who retain old rules, or receive transitional protections — often defined by birth year or when they first became eligible for certain benefits. These situations aren't common, but for those who qualify, they can make a meaningful difference in the benefit amount, especially if an early-retirement reduction would otherwise be steep.

The takeaway: if your story doesn't match the standard "I worked full-time, then at some point decided to retire" pattern — if it involves periods of disability, unusual employment histories, or complex timing — don't assume the generic early-claiming reductions tell the whole story. It's worth asking Social Security directly, or working with a knowledgeable planner, to explore whether any special rules apply to your specific situation.

Uncommon Benefit Situations: Divorced Spouses and Multiple Benefits

Divorce and multiple potential benefit entitlements add another layer of complexity to the Social Security playbook — but they also create real opportunities for income streams a lot of people never realize exist.

If you're divorced, as covered in Chapter 4, you may still be able to claim benefits based on your ex-spouse's work record, provided certain conditions are met. Typically, you need to have been married at least 10 years, be currently unmarried, and be at least 62 for spousal benefits, or at full retirement age for an unreduced benefit. In some circumstances your ex-spouse doesn't even need to have claimed their own benefit yet, though they do need to be eligible to do so. Crucially, your divorced-spouse benefit never reduces what your ex-spouse, or their current spouse, receives. Social Security isn't dividing a single pot between households — it's using the same earnings record to support more than one eligible person at once.

Similarly, if you're the surviving divorced spouse of someone who has died, you may qualify for survivor benefits based on their record, again subject to conditions around the length of the marriage, your current marital status, and your age. Survivor benefits can start as early as 60 (or 50 if disabled), though claiming early still triggers a reduction compared to waiting.

Where this gets especially interesting from a planning perspective is when someone qualifies for more than one type of benefit at once. You might have your own worker benefit from your employment, a divorced-spouse benefit from an ex, and perhaps a survivor benefit if your ex has since died. Social Security won't pay you all three simultaneously. Instead, the system evaluates each one and pays you essentially the highest amount you're entitled to, subject to coordination rules. In some situations, you may start with one type — a reduced survivor benefit, say — and later switch to your own worker benefit once it becomes larger at an older age.

For married couples, divorcees, and widows or widowers alike, these rules can significantly change the income picture from the basic claiming strategies covered in earlier chapters. A divorced person who thought they had only a small worker benefit might discover they can receive a much larger divorced-spouse benefit instead. Conversely, someone expecting to "collect on an ex" may learn their own worker benefit is actually higher — meaning they really just needed to focus on maximizing their own Social Security record all along.

The key step is inventorying all your potential claim bases: your own record, your current spouse, any ex-spouses, and any deceased spouses. Then consider timing — which benefit is largest at different ages, and how do early filing reductions or delayed retirement credits affect the trade-offs? Not every situation allows for creative sequencing, but some genuinely do, and the payoff for getting it right can be substantial over a retirement that may last 20 to 30 years.

Special Cases: Military Service, Railroad Retirement, and Federal Employees

Finally, some work histories intersect with separate retirement systems entirely, each with its own rules, and its own way of coordinating — or not coordinating — with Social Security.

Military service, for example, often earns credits that count toward Social Security in addition to a separate military retirement benefit. In many eras, active-duty pay was subject to Social Security tax, and certain periods of service generated extra deemed wage credits inside Social Security's own records. This means a career military member might receive a military pension and a full Social Security benefit simultaneously, without any WEP-type reduction, because their military work was covered by Social Security all along. That said, some reservist pensions based on specific non-covered service have been treated differently. It's worth confirming whether Social Security taxes were actually withheld on your particular type of service.

Railroad workers fall under yet another system entirely: the Railroad Retirement program. Railroad Retirement benefits are divided into tiers, with Tier I benefits designed to parallel Social Security, and Tier II benefits functioning more like a private pension. The Railroad Retirement Board coordinates with Social Security so your combined benefits follow specific formulas. Generally, you can't collect full Social Security benefits in addition to a full Tier I railroad benefit, because Tier I already substitutes for Social Security in that context. However, you might still be entitled to Social Security benefits based on non-railroad employment you had before, during, or after your railroad career, and those earnings can factor into the calculation.

Federal employees represent a third major special case. Those hired before 1984 were often covered by the Civil Service Retirement System (CSRS), a non-covered pension system that didn't include Social Security coverage at all. Historically, a lot of these workers were subject to both WEP on their own Social Security benefits, and GPO on spousal and survivor benefits. Those hired after 1983, under the Federal Employees Retirement System (FERS), paid Social Security taxes and generally weren't subject to either WEP or GPO on their federal pensions. After the repeal of WEP and GPO, the key planning issue is no longer whether those offsets apply at all — it's how Social Security coordinates with the worker's pension, savings, taxes, and survivor-income planning going forward.

State and local government employees, as you've seen throughout this chapter, occupy a genuinely wide range of situations, depending on whether their particular employer opted into Social Security coverage, and when. Teachers in one state may have sat entirely outside the system, while teachers in another state paid Social Security taxes all along. Police officers in one city might be exempt, while their counterparts in a neighboring jurisdiction are fully covered. Add in potential foreign employment for multinational workers, and the need for careful, case-by-case analysis becomes obvious.

For all of these special systems, the principle stays the same: don't assume your experience will match that of friends or family members who worked in more conventional, fully covered jobs. Always ask: Was this job covered by Social Security? Did I pay FICA taxes? Does my pension come from non-covered work? If so, how does that interact with WEP, GPO, or coordination rules like those in the railroad system — even after the 2025 repeal? Then integrate the answers into the broader planning framework laid out across the rest of this book: claiming age, tax planning, portfolio withdrawals, longevity risk, and estate goals.

As you move into subsequent chapters, which dig deeper into taxes, withdrawal strategies, and pulling all the pieces together into a coherent retirement income plan, keep this chapter in mind as your "exceptions manual." The basic rules are essential, but in real life, a lot of people have careers that cross borders — between public and private, covered and non-covered, healthy and disabled, married and divorced, domestic and foreign. The better you understand how these special provisions work, the more accurately you can forecast your income, and the more confidently you can choose a strategy that fits your real story, rather than a simplified textbook example.

The Bottom Line

If your career stayed entirely inside standard, fully-covered private employment, most of this chapter is background knowledge you'll rarely need. But if any part of your career touched government work, teaching, public safety, the military, railroads, or a foreign pension system, this chapter is essential reading — and worth revisiting any time you receive an estimate or piece of advice that doesn't match what you expected. WEP and GPO are gone as of January 2024, which means a meaningful number of older estimates and older planning conversations are now simply out of date.

KEY TAKEAWAYS

• WEP and GPO were both repealed by the Social Security Fairness Act, effective for benefits payable January 2024 and later. If you have an older estimate or older advice that assumed either provision, revisit it — your real benefit may now be higher than you were told.

• WEP historically reduced your own Social Security benefit if you had a non-covered pension plus fewer than 30 years of substantial covered earnings. It never affected your pension itself, and never affected benefits paid to your spouse or children.

- GPO historically reduced spousal and survivor benefits by two-thirds of a non-covered pension amount — in many cases wiping the benefit out entirely. It never affected your own worker benefit.
- SSDI converts automatically and seamlessly into a retirement benefit at full retirement age, with no new application, no paperwork, and no change in the dollar amount at the moment of conversion.
- Military service, railroad retirement, and federal employment (CSRS vs. FERS) each carry their own coordination rules with Social Security. Always confirm whether a specific period of your work history was actually covered before assuming the standard rules apply.

Next up: how to turn everything you've learned so far into simple decision trees and checklists — practical tools for claiming with confidence, whether you're single, married, widowed, or divorced.

Chapter 9: Simple Decision Frameworks: Flowcharts and Checklists to Claim Confidently

Chapter at a Glance

What you'll learn in this chapter:

• How to build a personal claiming decision tree that turns dozens of rules into a simple sequence of yes/no questions

• Four scenario-specific checklists — for singles, couples, widows and widowers, and divorced claimants — you can actually use

• Templates for productive conversations with financial advisors and Social Security representatives

• A notes and follow-up system that keeps your Social Security planning from sliding into a vague cloud of half-remembered conversations

Estimated reading time: 24 minutes

> ***FIELD NOTE*** *Pilots use checklists not because flying is too complicated for an expert to remember, but because under pressure, in the moment, anyone can skip a step. Social Security decisions happen exactly once for most people, under real pressure, with real money on the line. If pilots need a checklist for something they do every day, you can use one for something you'll do exactly once.*

Deciding when and how to claim Social Security is one of those decisions that looks simple from a distance, but quickly turns into a tangle of questions the closer you get to actually filing. You may have already tried a few online calculators, read several articles, maybe even spoken with Social Security directly — and still come away feeling uncertain. You're not alone in that. There are thousands of pages of rules, dozens of special exceptions, and a lot of "it depends" answers scattered across every resource you'll find. The good news:

most of that complexity can be organized into a handful of predictable paths and critical checkpoints.

In earlier chapters, you explored how benefits get calculated, how health and longevity expectations affect the break-even math, and how taxes and other income sources fit together. Here, we shift from "learning the rules" to "making the decision." This chapter is about equipping you with simple, structured tools — flowcharts, decision trees, and checklists — that help you move from confusion to an actual, actionable claiming plan. Think of it as turning a messy pile of puzzle pieces into the picture on the box that shows you exactly where everything goes.

These tools aren't meant to replace personalized advice, or the detailed analysis covered in the chapters on taxes, longevity, and withdrawals. Instead, they help you ask better questions, catch issues you might otherwise miss entirely, and walk into meetings with advisors or Social Security representatives already prepared. Structured tools like these are widely used in professional financial planning practice for exactly this reason — they help consistently navigate tricky questions and avoid costly oversights. Your version will be tailored to you, written in plain language, and genuinely usable at your own kitchen table.

In the sections ahead, we'll first look at claiming decision trees — flowchart-style paths that show how age, earnings, and special cases like divorce or widowhood steer you toward certain options. Then you'll work through scenario-based checklists for singles, couples, widows, widowers, and divorced individuals, letting you organize your steps without trying to hold everything in your head at once. Finally, you'll see templates and quick-reference tools that help you have genuinely productive conversations with financial planners, tax professionals, or Social Security representatives.

By the end of this chapter, you won't just know more — you'll have concrete tools to guide your next steps, and a repeatable process you can revisit any time your life changes.

9.1 Claiming Decision Trees: A Step-by-Step Guide

Doctors, pilots, and engineers rarely rely on memory alone for high-stakes decisions. They use checklists and flowcharts to keep their thinking orderly and reduce errors under pressure. The same approach works beautifully for Social Security. Put the rules into a visual decision tree — if yes, go this way; if no, go that way — and a pattern that felt overwhelming on the page suddenly becomes a lot easier to actually see.

Map Your Claiming Options Visually

A decision tree starts with a simple question, like "Are you at least age 62?" From there, each answer leads to another question: "Have you reached your full retirement age?" "Are you still working?" "Are you married right now?" Follow each branch, and confusing rules turn into a guided sequence of yes/no checkpoints, one at a time.

Imagine a basic retirement-benefit decision tree for someone considering their first claim:

1. Are you age 62 or older?

2. Have you reached your full retirement age?

3. Are you still working, and expecting earnings above the annual earnings limit?

4. Are you married, or divorced after a 10-year marriage?

5. Do you expect to live at least into your late seventies, based on your health and family history?

On paper, each question becomes a node with arrows pointing toward what to consider next. Answer "No" to the first question, and the tree simply says, "You're not yet eligible to claim retirement benefits. Focus on your earnings history and planning." Answer "Yes," and it directs you to the FRA question, and so on down the line.

The advantage of organizing your choices visually is that you don't have to hold every special rule in your head simultaneously. You only need to answer one question at a time. Instead of staring at a table of claiming ages and percentages, you walk along a clearly labeled path. For readers without a technical or financial background, this style of thinking often resonates a lot faster than dense text or formulas ever will.

This is exactly why professional planning tools — and a lot of educational sites — lean so heavily on charts and visual comparisons. Bar graphs, timelines, and simple trees help people see at a glance what they might gain or give up by claiming earlier or later. Your personal decision tree can be a lot simpler than those professional tools, and still be just as effective for your own purposes.

Incorporate Key Factors like Age and Earnings

Two factors dominate most claiming decisions: how old you are when you start, and how much you're working — and earning — at that time. The decision trees in this chapter organize their main branches around these two variables specifically.

Age comes first. One branch of your tree separates "Before FRA" from "At or After FRA." Claiming before FRA permanently reduces your monthly benefit, as covered in Chapter 2, while claiming after FRA increases it through delayed retirement credits. A typical tree might pose questions such as:

- "Are you at least age 62 but younger than your FRA?"
- "Have you reached FRA but are younger than 70?"
- "Are you 70 or older and not yet claiming?"

Each age band points you in a different direction. For someone still working and under FRA, the tree routes through the earnings test: "Do you expect to earn more than the annual limit this year?" Answer yes, and it flags the potential for part of your benefit to be withheld, suggesting you estimate whether claiming early is even worth it, given the reduction. Answer no, and it guides you to compare early-claiming reductions against your spending needs and longevity expectations instead.

Earnings come next. The trees also pay close attention to whether you'll keep working after claiming. Weaving this in prevents you from overlooking the earnings test or the tax impact of combining wages with Social Security — exactly the territory covered in Chapters 6 and 7. You saw how earnings above the limit can trigger withholding if you're under FRA, and how higher total income can push more of your benefit into the taxable range. In the tree, these become checkpoints like:

- "Will your wages or self-employment income exceed the annual earnings limit?"
- "Will your combined income from wages, Social Security, and other sources likely exceed the thresholds that cause up to 85% of your benefits to be taxable?"

Answer these questions honestly, and you can see a lot more clearly whether you should delay, whether a partial retirement strategy makes sense, or whether a spouse should claim first while the higher earner waits. This reflects the kind of structured analysis advisors run using professional software — just boiled down into plain-English pathways you can use yourself.

Because these trees are age- and earnings-centric, they also force you to think through transition periods: the year you cut your hours, the point when pensions start, the date you might sell a property and realize a large gain. As covered in the tax-aware claiming chapter, those transitions can meaningfully shift which claiming age is genuinely most attractive for you.

Highlight Important Exceptions and Special Cases

Not everyone fits neatly into a "working versus not working" retirement-benefit choice. Survivor benefits, divorced-spouse rules, and disability decisions all add layers your trees need to respect. Rather than hiding these special cases in footnotes, effective flowcharts call them out as distinct paths from the very start.

A survivor-benefits decision tree might begin with: "Has your spouse or ex-spouse, who was insured under Social Security, died?" Answer yes, and the next branches look genuinely different from someone considering only their own retirement benefit. You might be directed to questions such as:

• "Are you age 60 or older (or 50 with a qualifying disability)?"

• "Are you caring for a child under 16, or a disabled child receiving benefits on your late spouse's record?"

• "Have you remarried, and if so, at what age did you remarry?"

For divorced spouses, a separate path might ask whether your marriage lasted at least 10 years, and whether you're currently unmarried. Answer "Yes" to both, and you're directed to evaluate benefits based on your ex-spouse's record. Answer "No," and you stay on your own-record path instead.

Some exceptions involve coordination with disability benefits too. As covered in Chapter 7, individuals with serious health conditions before their FRA may be choosing between applying for disability insurance and taking a reduced retirement benefit instead. A decision tree for someone in this situation might include checkpoints such as:

• "Have you stopped working due to a health condition expected to last at least 12 months?"

• "Have you discussed potential disability eligibility with Social Security?"

Answer yes, and the tree may suggest exploring disability first, since an approved disability claim can effectively convert into a higher retirement benefit once you reach your FRA — exactly the mechanism explained in Chapter 8.

By explicitly marking these exception paths, you reduce the risk of accidentally following a "standard retiree" route when you actually qualify for a special rule. Instead of being a footnote, your specific circumstances become the main branch of your own tree.

Include Outcome Summaries at Decision Endpoints

The most useful decision trees don't simply say, "You should likely delay," or "You should consider claiming now." They translate those recommendations into concrete, money-related outcomes. At each endpoint — where no further questions remain — summarize exactly what following that path probably means in practice.

An outcome summary might include:

• An estimated monthly benefit at the chosen age.

• A brief note on whether benefits will likely be partly or mostly taxable.

• A reminder about survivor implications for a spouse.

• Any major trade-offs — for example, "You get more income now, but substantially less if you live past age 82."

Professional tools often present these comparisons as bar charts of annual benefits and cumulative lifetime totals. You can mimic that same clarity with a simple table or written summary next to each endpoint. For instance:

"Path A: Claim at 62 while still working part-time. Estimated monthly benefit: $1,400 (adjusted for early claiming). Because your wages plus this benefit exceed the earnings limit, expect part of your benefit to be temporarily withheld until you reach FRA. Combined income suggests up to 85% of benefits may be taxable. The survivor benefit for your spouse will be based on this reduced amount."

"Path B: Delay to age 67 (FRA). Estimated monthly benefit: $2,000. No early-claiming reduction. Easier to manage the earnings test if you're fully or mostly retired. Higher base for survivor benefits. This option requires savings or other income to cover the gap between ages 62 and 67."

Writing these outcomes in plain language helps you connect the abstract rule — "reduced by 30% at age 62 if FRA is 67" — to your actual lifestyle. You can then share these summaries with a financial planner or tax professional to refine the numbers further, without losing the overall logic you've already clarified for yourself.

These decision trees are meant to be living tools. As your work, health, or family situation changes, revisit your path and update your answers. In that sense, they connect directly to the ongoing planning process you encountered in earlier chapters on retirement income design and risk management. The tree doesn't lock you in — it simply keeps your thinking systematic as life genuinely unfolds.

9.2 Scenario-Based Checklists for Different Life Stages

While decision trees guide your thinking, checklists guide your actions. Surgeon and author Atul Gawande demonstrated how simple checklists dramatically reduced surgical errors, even among highly trained professionals operating in their area of expertise. Financial planners now use similar tools to make sure every critical step gets covered for each type of client. You can apply the exact same idea to your own Social Security decisions.

The key is using checklists that genuinely fit your situation. A single person faces different questions than a couple coordinating spousal and survivor benefits. A widow or widower faces different timing choices than someone divorced after a long marriage. In this section, you'll find scenario-based checklists you can adapt to your own life. Use them in sequence — work through what applies right now, then revisit them if your marital or family status changes down the road.

Singles: Key Steps to Avoid Common Pitfalls

For single individuals, Social Security decisions can seem simpler at first glance — there's no spouse's record to coordinate with. Yet a lot of singles underestimate how much flexibility they actually have, and how their choices affect long-term security. This checklist emphasizes thoroughness and awareness of the special rules that still apply.

Checklist for Single Claimants

Review your full work history and confirm your earnings record is correct on your Social Security statement.

Obtain benefit estimates for multiple claiming ages (62 through 70), and write them down side by side.

Evaluate your expected retirement budget, and determine how much of it Social Security will cover at each age.

Consider your health status and family longevity; note whether you're likely to live beyond your late seventies.

Model a "delay" strategy where you postpone claiming past your FRA, and compare the higher benefit to your savings drawdown.

Decide whether you plan to work while receiving benefits; if so, check the earnings test thresholds and implications.

If you've ever been married, confirm whether the marriage lasted at least 10 years and whether you're currently unmarried.

If previously married, ask Social Security whether a divorced-spouse or survivor benefit on an ex-spouse's record could exceed your own benefit.

Note any pensions from non-covered employment that may have affected older estimates or prior advice under the former WEP or GPO.

Create a simple "backup plan" in case your health or employment changes unexpectedly — for instance, how you'd adjust if you needed to claim earlier than planned.

Singles often underappreciate how powerful delaying can be, precisely because they don't have a spouse to "protect." Yet a higher personal benefit later in life can be your single strongest hedge against longevity and rising healthcare costs. If you have serious health concerns, you may reasonably decide that claiming earlier is appropriate — this checklist simply ensures you're making that trade-off consciously, rather than by accident.

Couples: Coordinating Claims for Optimal Household Income

For couples, the core question is rarely "When should each of us claim independently?" Instead, it's "How can we coordinate our choices to support our shared lifestyle and protect whichever of us survives the other?" Coordination is exactly where a lot of households leave real money on the table — often because both spouses claim early without fully realizing the long-term impact, as covered in Chapter 4.

Checklist for Married Couples

Gather both spouses' Social Security statements, and list each person's full retirement age and projected benefits at 62, FRA, and 70.

Identify which spouse has the higher primary insurance amount — the larger FRA benefit — since this will drive most survivor decisions.

Discuss your shared retirement timeline: when each of you plans to stop full-time work, and whether either of you will continue part-time.

Evaluate whether the lower earner might receive more by claiming a spousal benefit (up to 50% of the higher earner's FRA benefit) instead of their own.

Consider a strategy where the lower earner claims earlier (if needed for cash flow), while the higher earner delays claiming until FRA or age 70.

Estimate the surviving spouse's income under different scenarios: which benefit would continue, at what level, and how it would interact with other income sources.

Review the tax implications as a couple: how your combined benefits, retirement account withdrawals, and other income will be taxed, and how this changes once one spouse dies and the survivor becomes a single filer.

Check whether either spouse has a public pension from non-covered employment, and whether any older estimates or prior advice assumed a Government Pension Offset that no longer applies under current law.

Decide in advance how you'll adjust if markets perform poorly, or health changes — for example, whether the delaying spouse might move their claiming age forward.

Capture your agreed-upon strategy in writing, with target claiming ages, so both partners understand it and can revisit it together later.

This checklist builds directly on the couple-focused strategies you learned in Chapter 4. It encourages you to view Social Security as a household asset, rather than two separate checks that happen to land in the same account. By explicitly reviewing survivor implications and tax changes when filing status shifts, you meaningfully reduce the chance of unpleasant surprises years down the road.

Widows and Widowers: Navigating Survivor Benefits Efficiently

Losing a spouse is emotionally overwhelming, and financial tasks can feel far too complicated to handle on top of everything else. Yet Social Security survivor benefits are a vital income source for a lot of households, and a clear checklist can help you move through the process at your own pace while making sure important steps don't get missed.

Checklist for Widows and Widowers

Confirm that the death has been reported to Social Security (often done by the funeral home, but verify it yourself).

Ask Social Security about eligibility for the one-time $255 lump-sum death benefit, and whether you qualify.

Gather the required documents: your spouse's Social Security number, your own, the marriage certificate, the death certificate, and any prior divorce decrees if relevant.

Ask Social Security for an estimate of survivor benefits at different ages (starting at 60, or 50 if disabled, or any age if caring for a qualifying child).

Compare your own retirement benefit (current or future) with the survivor benefit; note which is larger at various ages.

Consider a "switching" strategy: for example, taking survivor benefits first and switching to your own higher retirement benefit later, or vice versa.

Evaluate the impact of continuing to work while receiving survivor benefits, including any earnings test issues if you're under your full retirement age.

If you're considering remarriage, review how the timing of remarriage could affect your survivor benefits; in many cases, remarriage after age 60 preserves eligibility.

Review the tax implications of moving from married-filing-jointly to single status, including how this affects the taxation of your Social Security benefits.

If your spouse had multiple sources of retirement income, coordinate survivor benefits with life insurance, pensions, and retirement accounts to create one coherent income plan.

Keep detailed notes of every conversation with Social Security, including names, dates, and any follow-up documentation requested.

Survivor benefit decisions are tightly linked to your broader post-loss financial picture. This checklist gives you a structured way to act on that knowledge one step at a time, rather than feeling like you have to solve everything at once during an already difficult period.

Divorced Individuals: Unlocking Benefits Beyond Your Marriage

Divorce doesn't necessarily sever your link to Social Security benefits based on a former spouse's record. If certain conditions are met, you may be entitled to spousal or survivor benefits even years after the marriage ended. A lot of divorced individuals never realize they qualify at all — a targeted checklist can help uncover those opportunities before it's too late to use them.

Checklist for Divorced Claimants

Confirm the duration of your marriage to each ex-spouse; note any marriage lasting at least 10 consecutive years.

Verify that you're currently unmarried, or, if remarried, understand how that affects your eligibility to claim on an ex-spouse's record.

Gather documentation, including divorce decrees, marriage certificates, and your ex-spouse's Social Security number, if known.

Ask Social Security whether you qualify for divorced-spouse benefits (up to 50% of your ex-spouse's FRA benefit), and for divorced-survivor benefits if your ex-spouse has died.

Compare the benefit you could receive on your own record with the divorced-spouse or divorced-survivor benefit; determine which is larger at relevant ages.

Clarify whether your ex-spouse's claiming decision affects you; often it doesn't, as long as they're eligible, but confirm this directly.

If you have multiple qualifying ex-spouses, ask which record provides the highest benefit, and whether you can switch between them.

Review how claiming on an ex-spouse's record affects your ability to switch to your own higher retirement benefit later, if applicable.

Confirm that your claim won't reduce your ex-spouse's benefits, or their current spouse's benefits; understanding this can reduce a lot of unnecessary emotional hesitation.

This checklist underscores that your Social Security story isn't limited to your current marital status. By verifying the duration of your marriage, your current marital status, and the possible survivor paths available to you, you increase the odds of receiving the highest benefit you're genuinely entitled to.

9.3 Templates and Quick Reference Tools for Advisor Conversations

Even with good decision trees and checklists in hand, you may still want professional guidance. Social Security is only one piece of your retirement puzzle, and integrating it with your investments, taxes, and estate plans often requires real expertise. At the same time, a meaningful amount of research has shown that a lot of people receive incomplete, or even incorrect, advice from various sources —

including well-meaning professionals who simply don't specialize in this area. Walking into those conversations organized and prepared makes it considerably more likely you'll receive accurate, genuinely personalized guidance.

In this section, you'll find templates you can adapt before meeting with a financial planner, tax adviser, or Social Security representative. These tools also connect back to earlier chapters — your retirement income projections, tax planning strategies, and healthcare considerations can all be summarized here, creating a compact dashboard for a genuinely productive conversation.

Personal Information and Benefits Summary Template

The first template is a simple summary sheet. It consolidates the key facts about you and your family that are relevant to Social Security decisions. Having all of this in one place speeds up meetings, and helps ensure no critical detail gets overlooked in the moment.

You might structure your summary like this:

• Basic information: your name, date of birth, current age, marital status, and citizenship or residency status.

• Work history snapshot: current employment, expected retirement date, approximate earnings for the current year, and whether you have any pensions from non-covered employment.

• Social Security record: full retirement age, estimated benefits at ages 62, FRA, and 70 from your statement, along with any notes about earnings corrections or open questions.

• Family status: information about your spouse or ex-spouse — names, dates of birth, marriage durations, divorce dates — children and their ages, and whether anyone has a qualifying disability.

• Health and longevity: brief notes on your health conditions, family longevity patterns, and whether you consider your expected lifespan shorter, average, or longer than typical, for planning purposes.

• Other income sources: pensions, annuities, rental income, expected portfolio withdrawals, and any major one-time events, such as selling a business.

Filling out this template forces you to gather exactly the kind of data online calculators and professional planning tools actually require. It also gives your adviser a clear starting point. Instead of spending the first half of a meeting pulling scattered details from memory, you can jump straight into evaluating real claiming scenarios.

Claiming Strategy Comparison Sheet

The second tool is a side-by-side comparison sheet for different claiming ages and strategies. Rather than trying to hold three or four options in your head at once, lay them out in simple columns. This approach mirrors the "lever" adjustments and scenario comparisons discussed in earlier chapters on retirement modeling.

A basic comparison sheet might include columns for:

• Strategy A: both spouses claim at 62 (or you claim at 62 if single).

• Strategy B: claim at FRA.

• Strategy C: delay until 70.

• Strategy D: coordinated couple strategy — for example, the lower earner claims at 62, while the higher earner delays until 70.

Under each column, record:

• Monthly benefit for each person (or for you alone, if single).

• Estimated annual household benefit.

• Percentage of benefits likely to be taxable, given your expected income.

• Expected survivor benefit for a spouse under that strategy.

• Notes on cash-flow implications in the early years — for example, "Requires drawing more from savings between 62 and 67."

• Break-even ages where delaying produces more lifetime income.

This kind of table invites a lot more systematic thinking. Instead of saying, "I feel like I should get something back as soon as I can," you can see, in tangible numbers, exactly what you trade off by claiming early or waiting. It also gives your financial planner or tax professional a clear structure for running calculations in their own software, and writing in refined numbers on top of your rough estimates.

The comparison sheet is also a direct bridge to the portfolio withdrawal strategies and tax bracket management ideas from Chapter 6. You can annotate each column with notes like "Allows Roth conversions from 62 to 67 in a lower tax bracket," or "Reduces required portfolio withdrawals early, preserving more for later years." Once you see these cross effects written down, Social Security stops feeling like an isolated decision and becomes a genuinely integrated part of your overall retirement plan.

Question Checklist for Social Security Representatives

Talking directly with Social Security can feel intimidating. Phone trees, wait times, and dense terminology don't make it easy. A question checklist helps you stay focused, and ensures you come away with answers that genuinely matter for your plan. Combined with the decision trees and scenario checklists from earlier in this chapter, you can use this list to verify your assumptions and clear up any remaining doubts.

Here's a sample question checklist you can adapt:

"Can you confirm my Full Retirement Age and my estimated benefits at 62, FRA, and 70 based on my current record?"

"Are there any earnings years missing or misreported on my record that I should correct?"

"If I claim before FRA while earning $X per year, how much of my benefit would be withheld under the earnings test?"

"Based on my marital and work history, am I eligible for any spousal, divorced-spouse, or survivor benefits? If so, what are the estimated amounts at different ages?"

"If I'm eligible for both my own retirement benefit and a spousal or survivor benefit, how would the claiming order work? Can I start with one and switch to the other later?"

"Would any Government Pension Offset or Windfall Elimination Provision rules apply to me because of my pension or my spouse's pension?" (Note: both were repealed effective January 2024, but it's still worth confirming how any older estimate you received may have been affected.)

"How do I officially change my claiming decision if I file and then decide I made a mistake — for example, within the first 12 months?"

"Can you explain how my benefits will be affected if I continue to work after reaching my Full Retirement Age?"

"What are the steps to apply for survivor benefits, and what documentation do I need to bring?"

"Where can I find written confirmation or publications that explain these rules, so I can review them later?"

Arriving with written questions helps you move beyond generic answers and straight into the specifics of your own case. It also aligns with how major advocacy organizations encourage people to interact with Social Security: prepared, focused, and persistent. Remember to take notes during the conversation, and ask the representative to spell their name and provide the date of the discussion for your own records.

Notes and Follow-Up Planner

The final tool is your glue: a notes and follow-up planner that keeps all the moving pieces together. As you talk with advisers, tax professionals, and Social Security staff, you'll accumulate recommendations, deadlines, and reminders like "we'll need to revisit this in two years." Without a simple system in place, those details can easily get lost in the noise of everyday life.

A practical planner might have sections such as:

• Meeting log: date, who you spoke with, and the main purpose of the meeting.

• Key takeaways: a short list of the most important conclusions or action items from that conversation.

• Next steps: tasks you or the professional agreed to complete — for example, "Submit corrected earnings information," "Run tax projections comparing claiming at 67 vs. 70," "Gather death certificate and marriage documents for survivor claim."

• Deadlines: specific dates, such as the last day to withdraw an early claim, the month you intend to file, or the target window for executing a particular tax strategy.

• Open questions: items that still need clarification, perhaps for a future meeting or phone call.

Using this planner transforms your Social Security journey from a vague cloud of information into a sequence of manageable actions. It connects back to the broader planning philosophy introduced earlier in this book: retirement isn't a one-time event, but an ongoing process of adjustment and refinement. By capturing each step, you build genuine confidence that you're not overlooking critical details along the way.

Putting it all together, the tools in this chapter — decision trees, scenario-based checklists, and advisor conversation templates — offer you a way to move through this entire process systematically. They don't claim to produce a single "perfect answer," because your life, health, and finances will keep evolving. But they meaningfully increase the chances that whatever decision you ultimately make about Social Security will be informed, intentional, and aligned with your broader retirement plan.

The Bottom Line

Complexity doesn't disappear just because you understand the rules — it disappears when you have a structured way to apply them to your own specific situation. A decision tree turns dozens of interacting rules into a sequence of simple questions. A scenario checklist makes sure you don't skip a step that matters specifically to your circumstances. And a few prepared questions, written down before you call Social Security or sit down with an advisor, turn a vague worry into a focused, productive conversation.

KEY TAKEAWAYS

• Decision trees work because they let you answer one question at a time, instead of holding every rule in your head simultaneously. Build yours around age, earnings, and the specific exceptions that actually apply to you.

• Use the checklist that matches your real situation — single, married, widowed, or divorced — rather than a generic one-size-fits-all list. Each carries genuinely different priorities and blind spots.

• Survivor and divorced-spouse checklists exist because these are exactly the benefits people miss most often. If you've been married 10+ years and divorced, or you've lost a spouse, work through the relevant checklist even if you think you already know your options.

• Prepare specific, written questions before any conversation with Social Security or a financial advisor. Vague questions get vague answers; specific questions get specific, usable numbers.

• Keep a simple notes and follow-up log for every Social Security conversation you have. Retirement planning spans years, and a written record protects you from having to relearn the same things twice.

Next up: how married couples can go beyond the basics and coordinate claiming sequences, survivor protection, and household assets together — the advanced playbook for peak lifetime income as a household.

Chapter 10: Advanced Coordination: Couples' Strategies for Peak Lifetime Income

Chapter at a Glance

What you'll learn in this chapter:

• Why the higher earner's claiming decision is the single most important Social Security choice most married couples will ever make

• The real difference between primary and spousal benefits, and why delayed credits never transfer to the spousal amount

• How to bridge the income gap while the higher earner delays — without derailing your savings

• How to weave pensions, IRAs, and other household assets into one coordinated income plan instead of treating Social Security as a standalone decision

Estimated reading time: 23 minutes

> ***FIELD NOTE*** *Couples almost always ask me the same question first: "When should we each claim?" It's the wrong question — not because it's unimportant, but because it treats two interconnected decisions as if they were separate. The real question is "How do we sequence our claims so the household, across both of our lives, comes out ahead?" That reframe changes almost everything that follows.*

Most couples approach Social Security with a deceptively simple question: "When should we each claim?" Hidden inside that innocent-sounding question, though, is a genuinely complex knot of rules around spousal, survivor, and individual benefits — and how you untie that knot can add or subtract tens of thousands of dollars from your lifetime household income. The stakes are high, not just for how comfortably you'll live in your 60s and 70s, but for how secure the surviving spouse will be if one of you dies first.

In earlier chapters, we focused mainly on individual strategies – understanding full retirement age, delayed credits, and the earnings test. Now we're going to zoom out, and treat you the way Social Security actually sees you: two separate workers sharing one financial life.

Your goal as a couple is bigger than simply making sure "each of us gets the most we personally can." The real objective is coordinating your choices so you meet cash-flow needs when work income falls, protect the larger benefit for as long as either of you might live, avoid tax and Medicare surprises, and integrate Social Security with pensions, IRAs, and other assets. Think of this chapter as the advanced playbook that builds on the foundations laid in earlier chapters about the basics, timing, and taxes. We'll move from sequencing decisions – who files first, and when – to survivor-focused strategies and income bridging, and finally to how your other retirement resources fit into the whole picture.

Throughout this chapter, keep one core principle in mind: for most married couples, the higher earner's claiming decision is the single most important Social Security choice they will make. That benefit becomes the default survivor benefit. If you take nothing else from this chapter, take that.

10.1 Coordinating Claiming Orders for Married Couples

When you're married, you don't just have two individual benefits – you also have options that connect your records: spousal benefits, survivor benefits, sometimes a restricted application for those who qualify, and a whole set of timing trade-offs. Claiming decisions stop being solely about age and money. They become about relationship dynamics, health, and shared risk.

Understanding the Impact of Primary vs. Spousal Benefits

Each spouse is entitled to a retirement benefit based on their own earnings record — their primary benefit. As covered in Chapter 1, this amount is determined by your highest 35 years of indexed earnings, then adjusted based on when you claim relative to full retirement age. Claim early, and your own benefit is permanently reduced. Delay past FRA, and you earn delayed retirement credits up to age 70, boosting your check by roughly 8% per year of delay.

On top of this, a lot of couples also have access to spousal benefits based on the other spouse's work record. At their own FRA, the maximum spousal benefit is up to 50% of their spouse's primary insurance amount — the benefit the spouse would receive if they claimed exactly at FRA. Importantly, that 50% is calculated on PIA, not on any delayed retirement credits the higher earner might eventually earn. So if one spouse builds their own benefit from a $2,000 PIA up to $2,640 by waiting until 70, the spousal maximum available to the other spouse is still based on the original $2,000 — never the $2,640.

Spousal benefits are also subject to early-claiming reductions of their own. Start a spousal benefit as early as 62, and it could be reduced to around one-third of your spouse's PIA. Unlike individual benefits, spousal benefits never increase if you delay claiming past your own full retirement age. Once you reach FRA, there's no further reward for waiting to start spousal benefits specifically. That distinction — delayed credits exist for your own benefit, but never for spousal benefits — is critical for coordination, and it's the single most commonly misunderstood point in this entire chapter.

In practice, you rarely see two separate checks labeled "your benefit" and "spousal benefit." Social Security uses what's sometimes called a "top-up" approach, exactly as covered in Chapter 4. They pay your own benefit first. If you're also eligible for a larger spousal benefit, they add a spousal "excess" amount on top, so you receive the higher of the two — never both in full. This prevents a common misconception: that a lower-earning spouse can collect 100% of their own benefit plus another full 50% as a spouse, stacked on top.

Because of these interacting rules, coordinating who claims first can significantly shift total household income. For some couples, leveraging a spousal benefit for the lower earner while the higher earner's own benefit keeps growing can smooth income and dramatically increase the long-term survivor benefit. For others — especially dual-earner couples with similarly sized records — spousal benefits matter a lot less, and the main decision simply revolves around each spouse's own optimal claiming age.

Optimal Claiming Sequences: Who Files First and When

Once you understand the difference between primary and spousal benefits, the next question is sequencing: who should file first? There's no single formula that fits every couple, but a few patterns show up again and again.

A common coordinating strategy: the lower-earning spouse claims earlier — sometimes as soon as they stop working, or reach their own FRA — while the higher-earning spouse delays, ideally until 70. The early claim by the lower earner starts cash flow moving, reduces the need to draw from savings, and may open up spousal benefits once the higher earner eventually files. Meanwhile, delaying the higher earner's benefit increases not just their own check while alive, but the survivor benefit that continues for as long as either spouse remains alive.

Consider a simplified example. Alex has a PIA of $3,000, and Jamie has a PIA of $1,000. Both claim at 62, and they lock in permanently reduced benefits — shrinking both current income and any future survivor benefit at the same time. Instead, suppose Jamie claims at 63 to bring some income into the household, while Alex waits until 70. Jamie's benefit is reduced, but Alex's check grows through delayed credits and cost-of-living adjustments. If Alex dies first, Jamie can step up to Alex's larger benefit as a survivor. Over a long joint lifetime — especially when one spouse is likely to outlive the other by a wide margin — the total dollars received can be a lot higher with this split-timing approach than with both claiming early.

Health and life expectancy play a decisive role here. If both spouses have strong family histories of longevity and are in good health, the extra years of higher benefits from delaying can outweigh the foregone income in their early 60s. If one or both spouses have serious health concerns or a shortened life expectancy, the calculus changes — taking benefits earlier can be a perfectly rational way to actually receive value from a system you've paid into your whole working life. In Chapter 2, we discussed life expectancy and break-even analyses for individuals. Here, the focus shifts to joint life expectancy — how long at least one of you is likely to live. A lot of couples underestimate this, because each partner tends to look only at their own prospects, forgetting that the survivor benefit gets paid for the longer of your two lifetimes, not the average.

Continued work is another factor worth flagging. If one spouse plans to keep working past 62, claiming benefits before FRA can trigger the earnings test from Chapter 7 and temporarily withhold benefits. That lost cash flow might undermine the entire point of claiming early in the first place. In a lot of couples, it makes sense for the spouse who's retiring earlier to consider claiming sooner, while the spouse who continues to earn should delay claiming — both to avoid earnings-test complications, and to keep building delayed credits in the meantime.

File and Suspend: An Advanced Strategy (Subject to Current Rules)

For years, "file and suspend" was an advanced strategy that let one spouse — usually the higher earner — file for benefits at their FRA, immediately suspend payments, and still allow the other spouse to claim a spousal benefit. The higher earner's own check would grow with delayed retirement credits, while the household collected a spousal benefit in the meantime. It was, for a while, one of the most popular advanced strategies in the entire system.

Law changes have significantly curtailed those opportunities, as covered briefly in Chapter 4. Under current rules, when you suspend your retirement benefit, all benefits payable on your record — including spousal benefits — are generally suspended too. You can't activate your benefit for your spouse while turning it off for yourself. The combination that once made file-and-suspend so attractive is mostly gone now.

That said, you may still encounter references to file and suspend online, or in older books, which can cause genuine confusion if you don't know the rules changed. The key takeaway: today, suspension is primarily about your own benefit. You can suspend between FRA and 70 to earn delayed credits if you regret an earlier claim, but your suspension will also halt benefits for anyone drawing on your record at the same time. If a professional or article suggests file and suspend as a way to trigger spousal payments while simultaneously enhancing your own benefit, double-check whether they're referring to outdated rules from before 2016.

A related, still-relevant concept is the restricted application, which we touched on in Chapter 9. If one spouse reached 62 by the end of 2015, they may still be eligible to file a restricted application at their FRA, allowing them to take only a spousal benefit while their own benefit continues to grow. The other spouse must have already filed. At 70, the spouse who filed the restricted application can switch over to their own enhanced benefit.

This can be extremely valuable, but it's limited to a shrinking cohort of older claimants. Because these advanced strategies rely on detailed eligibility conditions and laws that continue to evolve, it's wise to verify current rules before basing a long-term plan on them. The big picture, though, hasn't changed: the system increasingly nudges couples away from clever loopholes, and toward simpler trade-offs between early income and later, larger survivor-oriented benefits.

Considerations for Different Age and Earnings Gaps

No two couples look exactly alike on paper. Some are the same age with parallel careers; others are a decade apart in age, or have seen one spouse step away from paid work entirely for years at a time. Age gaps and income gaps both shape which strategies actually make sense for your household.

When one spouse is significantly younger, delaying the older, higher-earning spouse's benefit often becomes even more attractive than usual. The younger spouse is statistically more likely to end up the eventual survivor, so building the higher earner's benefit as large as possible strengthens the survivor income floor for what might be many years after the first spouse dies. Meanwhile, the younger, lower-earning spouse might use their own, smaller benefit earlier, particularly if they retire from paid work before the older spouse does.

Large disparities in earnings history also make spousal benefits more central to the whole plan. If one spouse has low or no earnings, spousal benefits may make up a major share of their retirement income. Because spousal benefits max out at 50% of the higher earner's PIA, and never earn delayed credits, the strategic focus usually shifts to two specific questions: when should the higher earner claim, to open the door to spousal benefits at all? And when should the lower earner claim, given that waiting past their own FRA never increases their spousal amount?

Often, the answer is that the higher earner should delay for the survivor benefit, while the lower-earning spouse claims as a spouse at or shortly after their own FRA. Coordinating around these differences requires honest conversations about goals, and about what "enough" income genuinely feels like. A couple who strongly values retiring together at 62 might accept lower long-term income, in exchange for more shared early-retirement years together. Another couple might prioritize the surviving spouse's security over maximum income in the first decade of retirement. The rules provide the constraints. Your values provide the direction.

10.2 Survivor Maximization and Income Bridging

Spousal benefits help while both of you are alive. Survivor benefits are what remain once one of you is gone. For a lot of couples — especially those with uneven earnings histories — planning with survivor benefits front and center is one of the most genuinely loving financial decisions you can make for each other.

Maximizing Survivor Benefits through Timely Claiming

Survivor benefits get misunderstood constantly. When a spouse dies, the surviving spouse may be eligible to step up to the higher of two benefits — either their own, or the deceased spouse's. At full survivor retirement age (which can differ slightly from the regular full retirement age), a surviving spouse can generally receive up to 100% of what the deceased spouse was receiving, or was entitled to receive, assuming basic eligibility conditions are met.

Here's the crucial link back to the claiming strategy covered earlier in this book: the deceased spouse's benefit at death is the starting point for the survivor benefit. Claim early and lock in a reduced benefit, and that smaller amount becomes the maximum survivor benefit, subject to a few special rules. Delay until 70 instead, and the larger benefit becomes the survivor's income base for the rest of their life.

This is exactly why Chapter 9 stressed that the higher earner's decision isn't just about their own personal life expectancy — it's about the life expectancy of either spouse. Delaying the higher earner's benefit functions like purchasing a lifetime, inflation-adjusted annuity for the surviving spouse — one that keeps paying as long as either of you is alive.

Planning to maximize survivor benefits does involve a real trade-off: you give up some income in your 60s, in exchange for considerably stronger protection in your 70s, 80s, and beyond. Couples uncomfortable with that trade-off sometimes choose a middle-ground approach — the higher earner delays at least until full retirement age, to avoid the early-claiming reduction entirely, while the lower earner claims earlier, supplying income during the waiting period. Others embrace a more aggressive stance, using other assets to fully bridge the gap until 70.

The right choice, again, depends on joint life expectancy, health, and available resources. If both spouses have modest savings and no other guaranteed income beyond Social Security, the temptation to claim early can be strong. Yet that's exactly when protecting the survivor may matter the most, because there are fewer backup assets to lean on later if the plan turns out wrong.

Using "Income Bridging" Strategies to Delay Social Security Claims

If you decide it's in your best interest — especially for survivor protection — to delay the higher earner's benefit, you need a genuine way to cover living expenses during the waiting period. That's where income bridging comes in. Instead of thinking, "We can't afford to delay," it helps to ask instead, "What could we actually live on while we wait?"

Bridging income often comes from other retirement assets. Traditional IRAs, 401(k)s, 403(b)s, and taxable investment accounts can all be tapped to create temporary income while you postpone claiming. Done thoughtfully, this approach can actually strengthen your long-term plan rather than weaken it. Spending down some pre-tax assets earlier may reduce your required minimum distributions later, which in turn can lower the share of your Social Security benefits that become taxable in your 70s and 80s — exactly the mechanism covered in Chapter 6.

A couple might, for example, plan to retire at 64, draw from a taxable brokerage account from 64 to 67, and then start the lower earner's Social Security while continuing modest portfolio withdrawals until the higher earner finally starts at 70. During this window, they might also execute Roth conversions at relatively low tax brackets, which not only improve future tax flexibility, but can also help keep later taxable income — and therefore Social Security taxation and Medicare surcharges — under control.

The key is treating Social Security and your portfolio as parts of one integrated system, not as separate silos that happen to coexist. A bridging strategy that looks, on the surface, like "spending assets faster" in the early years may, in fact, extend your portfolio's longevity and increase your lifetime after-tax income once the higher Social Security checks finally begin.

Coordinating Survivor and Spousal Benefits

Another layer of complexity shows up once you realize spousal benefits and survivor benefits operate under genuinely different rules. With spousal benefits, you're entitled to up to 50% of your spouse's PIA at your own FRA, and there's no advantage at all from your spouse's delayed credits. With survivor benefits, you may receive up to 100% of what your spouse was actually receiving or entitled to – including the full effect of any early or delayed claiming they did during their lifetime.

This distinction matters enormously for timing. Suppose the lower-earning spouse could access a spousal benefit once the higher earner files, but you're also concerned with maximizing the eventual survivor benefit. It might be tempting to have the higher earner file earlier, so the lower earner can access the spousal benefit sooner. But that early claim reduces the very benefit the surviving spouse may eventually rely on for decades. In a lot of cases, the smarter move is accepting a lower or delayed spousal benefit now, in order to protect the much larger future survivor benefit.

Survivor benefits also offer more flexibility around switching than standard spousal benefits do. A surviving spouse can, in some situations, claim one type of benefit – a reduced survivor benefit at 60, say – and later switch to their own retirement benefit at 70, if that turns out to be larger, or do the reverse instead. This "two-pots" concept can be genuinely powerful in age-gapped couples, where the widow or widower might significantly outlive the spouse who died.

Because the rules here are intricate – particularly around whether you're deemed to have filed for one type of benefit when you apply for another – using a reputable calculator, or working with a qualified advisor, can be genuinely invaluable. For now, remember simply that coordinating survivor and spousal benefits is not an area where guesswork is your friend.

Planning for Remarriage and Blended Family Situations

Real life rarely follows the neat pattern of one lifelong marriage. Divorce, remarriage, stepchildren, and complicated family trees can all affect your Social Security options. In Chapter 4, we introduced divorced-spouse benefits and ex-spouse survivor rules; now let's look at how those interact with married-couple coordination specifically.

One key rule worth repeating: survivor benefits from a deceased spouse generally stop if the widow or widower remarries before age 60 (or 50 if disabled). Remarrying after that age typically preserves survivor eligibility. That timing nuance can matter enormously for anyone widowed in their 50s and considering remarriage — the decision carries emotional, legal, and financial layers all at once, and Social Security is genuinely one of them, whether or not it feels appropriate to weigh it at the time.

Blended families can introduce additional complexity too. Stepchildren may qualify for certain family benefits based on a stepparent's record, if specific conditions are met. Ex-spouses may already be drawing divorced-spouse benefits, or survivor benefits, based on a worker's record. The good news: in a lot of cases, benefits paid to ex-spouses or children don't reduce what's payable to the current spouse. They do, however, add administrative complexity, and sometimes lead to misconceptions within families about who is "taking" from whom — misconceptions that usually aren't accurate.

For couples entering a second or later marriage, it's genuinely wise to map out how existing and potential Social Security rights intersect: who has credits from a prior marriage, how remarriage might change survivor eligibility, and how joint claiming choices might affect adult children or disabled dependents. A bit of planning here can help you avoid painful surprises — a survivor benefit disappearing that you'd counted on, or a remarriage unintentionally disqualifying you from a favorable claiming path on an ex-spouse's record.

10.3 Integrating Pensions, IRAs, and Other Assets with Social Security

So far in this chapter, we've focused mainly on Social Security's own rules. But your retirement reality is broader than that — pensions, employer plans, IRAs, annuities, rental properties, and brokerage accounts all contribute to your household's cash flow. The most effective couples' strategies weave Social Security decisions together with all of these other income sources, rather than treating Social Security as a decision made in isolation.

Coordinating Pension Payouts with Social Security to Avoid Income Cliffs

Traditional pensions are becoming rarer, but a lot of couples still have at least one defined benefit plan from government, education, or older corporate employment. Pensions can be structured in many ways: single-life only, joint-and-survivor options, or designs that change once Social Security eligibility ages are reached. Some have explicit offsets tied to Social Security; others simply stack on top, with no interaction at all.

The first step is understanding any pension provisions that interact directly with Social Security. Some employer plans reduce the pension once Social Security begins; others integrate with your Social Security earnings history when determining the benefit formula in the first place. Although WEP and GPO were repealed by the Social Security Fairness Act, as covered in Chapter 8, the broader message remains the same: know exactly how your specific pension coordinates with Social Security, taxes, survivor income, and the rest of your retirement plan.

Timing matters considerably here. Suppose one spouse has a pension that can start as early as 60, and both spouses plan to delay Social Security. Starting that pension earlier could provide the income needed to bridge the Social Security delay, reducing pressure on your portfolio in the meantime. Alternatively, if both Social Security and the pension are set to begin in the same year, you might find yourself leaping from modest income straight to a high combined income that pushes you into a higher tax bracket, and potentially triggers Medicare premium surcharges a couple of years later.

One effective approach is staggering start dates, so new income sources phase in gradually over time. Start a pension when the first spouse retires, delay the higher earner's Social Security until 70, and only later begin required minimum distributions from retirement accounts. By smoothing these transitions deliberately, you avoid the harsh "income cliffs" where your tax bill suddenly jumps in a single year, catching you off guard.

Smart IRA and 401(k) Withdrawals to Optimize Tax Efficiency

In Chapter 6, we described how Social Security gets taxed based on "combined income" — provisional income, in the terminology we used there — which includes half of your Social Security benefits plus other income, like wages, taxable interest, and distributions from traditional IRAs and 401(k)s. For couples, these rules interact with both spouses' benefits and withdrawals simultaneously, sometimes in genuinely surprising ways.

Coordinated withdrawals — especially before both spouses are drawing full Social Security — can create valuable flexibility. If you choose to delay the higher earner's benefit, the early retirement years may be an excellent time to take larger withdrawals from pre-tax accounts, while you're still sitting in relatively low tax brackets. Later, once both Social Security checks are flowing and required minimum distributions kick in, you'll be glad you already reduced those account balances ahead of time.

Managing the timing and amount of IRA and 401(k) withdrawals carefully can help keep your combined income below the key thresholds where more of your Social Security becomes taxable, or where you cross into higher Medicare premium brackets. You might intentionally keep taxable income within a specific band to avoid having 85% of your benefits taxed, for instance. Or you might coordinate Roth conversions with years when only one spouse is receiving benefits, taking advantage of the temporary "tax valley" between full-time work and full retirement income.

Think of this as a three-dimensional puzzle: your claiming ages, your withdrawal strategy, and your tax brackets all interact across many years simultaneously. You're not just maximizing raw Social Security benefits — you're maximizing after-tax, inflation-adjusted cash flow, which is what actually funds your lifestyle day to day.

Using Other Income Sources to Facilitate Delayed Social Security Claiming

Beyond pensions and retirement accounts, a lot of couples have other income sources that can be harnessed to support a delay-and-protect strategy. Ongoing work, consulting, or part-time jobs can provide cash flow. Rental properties can generate regular income. Small business income, royalties, or phased retirement arrangements with an employer can all create a genuine financial bridge while the higher earner waits.

If one spouse enjoys their work and expects to continue into their late 60s, that can justify delaying that spouse's Social Security all the way to 70, while the other spouse retires earlier and perhaps claims benefits at or near their own FRA. The working spouse's earnings fill the income gap and reduce the need for withdrawals elsewhere, while the delayed Social Security benefit quietly builds survivor protection in the background.

Of course, there are trade-offs. Working longer may come with stress, health impacts, or missed opportunities for shared leisure time together. Couples need to weigh the value of higher guaranteed income later, against the very real, non-financial benefits of retiring together, or simply reducing work sooner rather than later. There's no universally wrong answer here — only the answer that best reflects your own shared priorities as a couple.

When weighing these trade-offs, it genuinely helps to run side-by-side projections: What does our lifetime income look like if we both stop working and claim benefits at 62? What if one of us works three more years, and we delay one benefit until 70? What if we bridge those years with a mix of part-time work and portfolio withdrawals instead? The seeds of that comparison thinking belong right here, even though we'll explore fuller scenario planning in later chapters.

Building a Comprehensive Household Cash Flow Plan

Ultimately, Social Security is one thread in the fabric of your retirement — an important one, but still just one. To genuinely benefit from advanced coordination, you need a comprehensive household cash flow plan that integrates all your income sources at once. Instead of asking, "What should we do about Social Security?" in isolation, ask instead: "How do Social Security, pensions, IRAs, and other assets work together to provide the income we want, at an acceptable level of risk, for as long as either of us is alive?"

Start by mapping expected income year by year, from every source: each spouse's Social Security under various claiming ages, pension start dates, required minimum distributions, any annuity income, rental income, and planned part-time work. Visualize all of this as a timeline, so you can see clearly where income is naturally abundant, and where genuine gaps appear. Those gaps are exactly where your claiming decisions and withdrawal strategies do the most work.

Next, factor in taxes and healthcare costs. A higher combined income in some years will increase both your income tax and, potentially, your Medicare premiums. Sometimes, slightly lowering your gross income by delaying or staggering income sources actually results in higher net income, because you avoid these hidden costs entirely. Other times, you may deliberately accept a tax spike for one year, to achieve a larger long-term benefit — a major Roth conversion, say, or a clean transition from full-time work into full retirement.

Finally, commit to revisiting this plan regularly. Life happens: health changes, markets fluctuate, work opportunities arise or disappear, and laws continue to evolve, exactly as they did with the Social Security Fairness Act in 2025. A plan built at 60 may genuinely need adjustment at 65, at 70, or after a major life event neither of you anticipated. The coordination strategies covered in this chapter aren't a one-time decision — they're part of an ongoing process of fine-tuning your household's retirement engine, year after year.

As you move into the chapters ahead, we'll build on this coordinated framework — exploring how to run realistic scenarios, how to stress-test your plan against market and longevity risk, and how to adapt if your initial claiming choices no longer fit. For now, remember that as a couple, you hold a genuinely powerful lever: by coordinating timing, survivor protection, and integration with your other assets, you can transform Social Security from a simple monthly check into a carefully engineered foundation for your entire retirement story.

The Bottom Line

Married couples have more levers to pull than singles, but only if they pull them together rather than separately. The higher earner's claiming decision sets the survivor's income floor for potentially decades, which makes it the single most consequential choice in this entire chapter. Bridge the gap with savings, a pension, or continued work if you can — the near-term sacrifice usually pays for itself many times over in long-term household security.

KEY TAKEAWAYS

• Spousal benefits cap at 50% of the higher earner's PIA — not their delayed-credit-boosted benefit — and never grow if the spouse delays claiming past their own FRA. Survivor benefits, by contrast, can reach up to 100% of the deceased's actual benefit, including any delayed credits they earned.

• The most common effective sequence: the lower earner claims earlier for near-term cash flow, while the higher earner delays — ideally to 70 — to maximize both their own benefit and the eventual survivor benefit.

• File-and-suspend, as it once worked, is mostly gone since 2016. Restricted applications still exist, but only for people who reached 62 by the end of 2015 — verify current rules before planning around either strategy.

• Income bridging — using savings, a pension, or continued work to cover expenses while the higher earner delays — often strengthens the long-term plan rather than weakening it, partly by reducing future RMDs and the taxation that comes with them.

• Social Security decisions shouldn't be made in isolation. Map pensions, IRA withdrawals, and other income sources alongside your claiming ages to avoid tax-bracket and Medicare-surcharge "income cliffs," and revisit the whole plan regularly as life changes.

Next up: real-world case studies showing exactly how these principles play out for different people — a single early claimer, a couple coordinating spousal strategy, a high earner managing taxes, and a divorced claimant discovering benefits she never knew she had.

Chapter 11: Real-World Case Studies: Learn from Practical Examples

Chapter at a Glance

What you'll learn in this chapter:

• Four detailed profiles — a single retiree, a married couple, a high-earning consultant, and a divorced claimant — showing how the same rules produce different right answers

• The most common, costly mistakes real claimants make, and the specific fix for each one

• Side-by-side dollar comparisons showing exactly what coordination, delay, or a missed benefit is worth over a lifetime

• How to map your own situation onto these profiles, even if your numbers don't match exactly

Estimated reading time: 26 minutes

> ***FIELD NOTE*** *Every mistake in this chapter's "common mistakes" section was made by someone who had access to all the same information you now have. None of them were careless people. They simply never sat down and ran the numbers before filing — because nobody told them that's what you're supposed to do before a decision this size.*

Reading about Social Security in the abstract — percentages, formulas, bend points — only gets you so far. At some point, the rules need to meet a real life: a real age, a real health history, a real spouse, a real set of savings. This chapter exists to make that connection. We'll walk through four claiming profiles built from situations that mirror what real people actually face, then look honestly at the mistakes that show up again and again, and finally compare the dollar outcomes side by side so the stakes feel concrete rather than theoretical.

As you read, resist the urge to look for a profile that matches you exactly. None of them will. Instead, look for the pattern underneath each story — the break-even thinking, the survivor protection, the tax awareness, the overlooked benefit — and ask how that same pattern might apply to your own numbers, your own health, your own family. That's the actual skill this chapter is teaching: not memorizing four examples, but learning to think the way these four people eventually learned to think.

11.1 Case Study: Single Retiree Claiming at Different Ages

Jane represents one of the most common situations in this entire book: a single person trying to decide whether claiming sooner or later actually serves her better. There's no spouse to coordinate with, no survivor benefit to protect — just Jane, her own work record, and a decision that will shape her income for the rest of her life.

Jane's Profile

Jane is 62, single, and ready to leave a demanding career that has worn her down over the past several years. Her full retirement age is 67, and her statement shows a projected benefit of $2,000 a month at that age. Claim now, at 62, and her benefit drops by roughly 30%, to about $1,400 a month. Wait until 70 instead, and delayed retirement credits push her benefit up to roughly $2,480 a month.

On the surface, $1,400 a month starting immediately feels appealing — especially after a stressful stretch at work. But Jane's parents both lived into their late 80s, she's currently in good health, and she has some savings along with the option to pick up part-time consulting work for a few years if she chooses to delay.

Running the Numbers

Jane decides to compare her total lifetime benefits under three claiming ages, assuming she lives to 90, and ignoring cost-of-living adjustments for simplicity.

Claim at 62 ($1,400/month): 28 years of payments × $16,800 per year = $470,400 total.

Claim at 67 ($2,000/month): 23 years of payments × $24,000 per year = $552,000 total.

Claim at 70 ($2,480/month): 20 years of payments × $29,760 per year = $595,200 total.

By age 90, the delayed strategy has produced roughly $125,000 more than claiming at the earliest possible age — and that gap would be even larger once realistic cost-of-living adjustments are factored in, since those increases apply to a larger base benefit every single year going forward.

Jane also calculates her break-even age between claiming at 62 and waiting until 70: somewhere around 79. Given her family history, she considers it reasonably likely she'll live well past that age. That tilts the math meaningfully in favor of waiting, at least from a pure lifetime-income perspective.

Jane's Decision

Jane ultimately decides to delay — not necessarily all the way to 70, but at least to 65, using occasional consulting work to bridge the gap and ease the financial pressure of waiting. The arrangement gives her flexibility: if her health changes, or consulting work dries up sooner than expected, she can revisit her plan and claim earlier than originally intended. If things go smoothly, she may stretch her delay closer to 70, capturing even more of the available upside.

Jane's story illustrates a theme worth carrying into your own thinking: the "right" claiming age isn't a fixed number you commit to forever the moment you turn 62. It's closer to a working hypothesis — one informed by real numbers, real health expectations, and real financial flexibility — that you're willing to revisit as your circumstances evolve.

11.2 Case Study: Married Couple Optimizing Survivor and Spousal Benefits

Bob and Linda show exactly how much is at stake when a married couple coordinates — or fails to coordinate — their claiming decisions. Their story isn't about complicated rules so much as it's about what happens when those rules go unexamined until it's too late to change course.

Bob and Linda's Profile

Bob has a full retirement age benefit of $2,400 a month. Linda's full retirement age benefit is $900 a month. Neither has a pension from non-covered work, so the standard claiming rules from earlier chapters apply cleanly to both of them.

Scenario One: No Coordination

In this version of their story, Bob and Linda each claim at 62, simply because that's the earliest age available and neither has thought much beyond that. Bob's benefit drops to roughly $1,680 a month. Linda's drops to roughly $630 a month. Combined household income: $2,310 a month while both are alive.

If Bob dies first — and given that he's the higher earner, his benefit is what Linda would step up to as a survivor — Linda's survivor benefit becomes $1,680 a month, the same reduced amount Bob locked in at 62. That's the number she'll need to live on, potentially for many years, on top of whatever else they've saved.

Scenario Two: Coordinated Claiming

In the coordinated version, Linda claims at her own FRA, receiving her full $900 a month. Bob delays all the way to 70, allowing his $2,400 PIA to grow through delayed retirement credits to roughly $2,976 a month. Combined household income once Bob reaches 70: $3,876 a month — considerably more than the uncoordinated scenario, even though it required patience and some bridging income in the meantime.

If Bob dies first in this version of the story, Linda's survivor benefit steps up to $2,976 a month — nearly $1,300 more per month than in the uncoordinated scenario. Over 15 years of survivorship, that $1,296 monthly difference adds up to roughly $233,000 in additional lifetime income for Linda alone, before any cost-of-living adjustments are even factored in.

The Real Lesson

Bob and Linda's comparison isn't really about whether $2,310 or $3,876 a month sounds better while both are alive — it's about what happens to whichever one of them is left. The coordinated strategy required some near-term sacrifice: tighter cash flow during the years Bob delayed, possibly some drawn-down savings or part-time work to bridge the gap. But the long-term payoff, concentrated specifically in the years when Linda might be living alone, is substantial enough that it's hard to ignore once you see the numbers side by side.

This is exactly the pattern described in Chapter 4 and Chapter 10: the higher earner's claiming decision is, in a very real sense, a decision made on behalf of whoever survives them. Bob and Linda's story is a reminder that this isn't an abstract principle — it's a six-figure difference, playing out over the back half of one person's life.

11.3 Case Study: High-Income Earner Managing Tax Implications

Carlos's situation looks different from Jane's and from Bob and Linda's. He doesn't face a stark early-versus-late trade-off, or a spousal coordination puzzle. His challenge is what happens when a healthy Social Security decision collides with an already complicated tax picture.

Carlos's Profile

Carlos is 67 — already at his full retirement age — single, and still earning substantial income from consulting work, alongside a healthy investment portfolio generating dividends and capital gains. His FRA benefit is $3,000 a month. If he delays until 70, his benefit grows to roughly $3,720 a month.

The Break-Even Math

Run the basic break-even calculation from Chapter 2: delaying from 67 to 70 means foregoing 36 months of $3,000, or $108,000 in total. In exchange, Carlos gains $720 a month for the rest of his life. Divide the foregone amount by the monthly gain, and the payback period comes out to about 150 months — just over 12 years. Add that to age 70, and Carlos's break-even age lands around 82, which is well within a reasonable expectation for a healthy 67-year-old.

On the surface, this looks like a fairly ordinary delay decision — reasonably attractive, not dramatically different from Jane's situation in section 11.1. But Carlos's actual decision hinges on something the simple break-even calculation doesn't capture at all: taxes.

The Hidden Tax Problem

Carlos's consulting income and investment income are already substantial on their own. As covered in Chapter 6, once his provisional income crosses certain thresholds, up to 85% of his Social Security benefit becomes taxable — and additional income on top of that can trigger a higher effective marginal rate than his stated tax bracket would suggest. If Carlos claims at 67 while still earning significant consulting income, he's effectively stacking a new $36,000-a-year income source directly on top of an already-high-income year, pushing a large share of his Social Security straight into the taxable zone with very little benefit to show for it.

By delaying to 70 instead, Carlos buys himself three additional years during which his taxable income — absent the new Social Security check — may still be manageable enough to execute Roth conversions at a reasonable rate. Those conversions shrink his traditional IRA balances, which in turn reduces his future required minimum distributions. Smaller future RMDs mean less pressure pushing his provisional income upward later, which means less of his eventual, larger Social Security check gets pulled into the 85% taxable zone once he finally does start collecting.

Carlos's Decision

Carlos decides to delay to 70 — not purely because of the break-even math, which was attractive but not overwhelming on its own, but because of what those three additional years let him do with the rest of his financial picture. The delay isn't just about a bigger check later; it's about restructuring his retirement income to be more tax-efficient overall, for decades to come.

Carlos's story is a useful corrective for anyone evaluating Social Security purely through the lens of "what's my break-even age?" That question matters, but as Chapter 6 explained in detail, it's incomplete on its own for higher earners with substantial other income. The tax consequences of claiming at a particular moment can meaningfully shift the calculus, sometimes in ways that strengthen the case for delay even further than the raw benefit numbers alone would suggest.

11.4 Case Study: Divorced Individual Navigating Benefit Options

Susan's story addresses a gap a lot of readers don't realize applies to them: the rights divorced individuals retain on an ex-spouse's earnings record. It's one of the most underused provisions in the entire system, almost always simply because people don't know it exists.

Susan's Profile

Susan is 66 and divorced after a 15-year marriage. Her own full retirement age benefit, based on her personal work history, is $900 a month. Her ex-husband's full retirement age benefit is $2,400 a month. Until recently, Susan had simply assumed her own $900 benefit was the only option available to her.

Discovering the Divorced-Spouse Benefit

As covered in Chapter 4, anyone married at least 10 consecutive years and now divorced may be eligible for a benefit based on their ex-spouse's record, as long as they're currently unmarried and meet the basic age requirements. Susan's 15-year marriage clears that bar comfortably.

Her divorced-spouse benefit is calculated the same way a current spousal benefit would be: up to 50% of her ex-husband's PIA, claimed at her own full retirement age. Half of his $2,400 PIA is $1,200 — considerably more than her own $900. At her FRA, Susan can claim the higher of the two amounts, and Social Security will pay her the $1,200 divorced-spouse benefit rather than her own smaller benefit. Critically, this claim has zero effect on her ex-husband's own benefit, or on the benefits available to his current spouse, if he's remarried.

A Second Layer: Divorced Survivor Benefits

Susan's situation has one more wrinkle worth understanding now, even though it hasn't happened yet. If her ex-husband eventually dies while she's collecting the divorced-spouse benefit, Susan may become eligible to switch to a divorced survivor benefit instead — potentially up to 100% of whatever he was receiving at the time of his death, subject to the usual rules around her own claiming age.

If her ex-husband delayed his own claim and was receiving something like $3,000 a month by the time he died, Susan's eventual survivor benefit could be considerably larger than the $1,200 divorced-spouse benefit she started with. This is exactly the kind of sequencing opportunity described in Chapter 4 and Chapter 10: one benefit type now, with the door open to a potentially larger benefit type later, depending on how events unfold.

Susan's Decision — and the Real Lesson

At her FRA, Susan claims the $1,200 divorced-spouse benefit rather than settling for her own $900. Over 20 years, that $300-a-month difference adds up to $72,000 she would otherwise have left unclaimed — not because of some complicated strategy, but simply because she didn't know the option existed until she went looking.

Susan's story is less about clever optimization and more about basic awareness. A meaningful number of divorced individuals never investigate whether they qualify for benefits on an ex-spouse's record, sometimes out of a vague sense that doing so would be "taking" something from their ex. It wouldn't have been, in Susan's case, and it generally isn't in anyone else's either. The lesson here is simple: if you've been married at least 10 years and are now divorced, this is a question worth asking directly, even if you assume the answer is no.

11.5 Common Mistakes and How to Avoid Them

The four profiles above each illustrate a productive decision-making process. But it's just as instructive to look at what happens when that process doesn't happen at all — when people default into a choice without examining it first. The following four mistakes show up again and again, in slightly different forms, across a huge range of real claimants.

Mistake One: Claiming Without Understanding the Reduction

Picture a version of Jane's story where she never ran the numbers from section 11.1. She turns 62, remembers that's the earliest age she can claim, and simply files — without comparing $1,400 a month against $2,000 at FRA or $2,480 at 70. She receives her reduced benefit, feels fine about it for the first several years, and doesn't think much more about it.

By her late 70s, though, inflation has eroded her purchasing power, healthcare costs have risen, and she finds herself wishing she had the $1,850 a month she would have received by waiting until 65 — a number that, in this version of her story, she never even calculated at the time. The decision was permanent the moment she filed, and there's no way back.

The fix isn't a blanket rule like "never claim at 62." As Jane's actual decision in section 11.1 shows, claiming early can be entirely appropriate for some people. The fix is simply running the comparison — break-even age, three benefit estimates side by side, a rough sense of your own budget — before you file, so that whatever you decide, you decided it on purpose.

Mistake Two: Failing to Coordinate as a Couple

This is exactly the uncoordinated version of Bob and Linda's story from section 11.2. Each spouse looks only at their own situation, claims whenever feels personally convenient, and never models what happens to the survivor specifically. When Bob dies at 78 in this version of events, Linda discovers her survivor benefit is the reduced $1,680 amount — not the larger number she'd vaguely assumed, without ever actually checking.

There is some ability to partially correct an early-claiming mistake after the fact. Within 12 months of filing, you can withdraw your application, repay the benefits you've received, and refile later as though you'd never claimed at all. After reaching FRA, you can suspend your benefit to let delayed credits accumulate going forward. Both tools are limited, though, and neither fully undoes years of reduced payments already received.

The better approach, as Bob and Linda's coordinated scenario demonstrates, is modeling the survivor outcome before either spouse files — not after. The specific question to ask is straightforward: "If one of us died next year, what would the survivor's Social Security income actually look like, under each claiming combination we're considering?" That conversation takes maybe twenty minutes, and it's twenty minutes that can be worth hundreds of thousands of dollars over a long widowhood.

Mistake Three: Ignoring Tax Implications

This mirrors an unplanned version of Carlos's story from section 11.3. Imagine Carlos claims at 67 without ever running a provisional income calculation, simply because he'd reached his full retirement age and it felt like the natural moment to start. He hadn't modeled what stacking a new Social Security check on top of his consulting and investment income would actually do to his effective marginal tax rate, or to his Medicare premiums two years later through the IRMAA surcharge system.

The fix, as Carlos's real decision shows, is running a rough provisional income calculation — AGI excluding Social Security, plus tax-exempt interest, plus half of the projected Social Security benefit — for the specific year benefits would start, before deciding when to claim. If that calculation shows you're already deep into the 85%-taxable zone from other income sources, claiming sooner rather than later may create more tax cost than the extra income is actually worth, at least for the years immediately following your claim.

Mistake Four: Missing Divorced-Spouse and Survivor Eligibility

This is simply Susan's situation from section 11.4, played out without the moment of discovery that changed her outcome. A lot of divorced individuals never ask whether they qualify for benefits on an ex-spouse's record — sometimes from a mistaken belief that doing so would reduce what the ex-spouse receives, sometimes simply because nobody ever suggested checking.

The fix costs nothing but a phone call or an online inquiry: if you were married at least 10 years and are now divorced, ask Social Security directly whether you qualify for divorced-spouse or divorced-survivor benefits, and what the estimated amounts would be at different ages. As Susan's story shows, the answer can be worth tens of thousands of dollars over a normal retirement — money that's already legally available to you, waiting only on the question being asked.

11.6 Side-by-Side Comparisons

Numbers tend to stick better when you can see two paths laid out next to each other, rather than scattered across several pages. Here are direct comparisons drawn from each profile above.

Jane: Three Claiming Ages at Age 90

Claim at 62 ($1,400/month): 28 years × $16,800/year = $470,400 total.

Claim at 67 ($2,000/month): 23 years × $24,000/year = $552,000 total.

Claim at 70 ($2,480/month): 20 years × $29,760/year = $595,200 total.

By age 90, the delayed strategy has produced roughly $125,000 more than the earliest claiming age — and every one of these totals would be higher in real terms once cost-of-living adjustments are layered onto the comparison, since those adjustments compound on a larger base benefit the longer you waited to claim.

Bob and Linda: Coordinated vs. Uncoordinated

Uncoordinated (both claim at 62): combined household income of $2,310/month while both are alive. Survivor benefit if Bob dies first: $1,680/month.

Coordinated (Linda at FRA, Bob at 70): combined household income of $3,876/month while both are alive. Survivor benefit if Bob dies first: $2,976/month.

The coordination decision is worth $1,296 a month to whichever spouse survives the other — over 15 survivor years, more than $230,000 in additional lifetime income, before any inflation adjustments are applied.

Carlos: Gross Benefit vs. After-Tax Reality

Claiming at 67 with high consulting income: Social Security becomes substantially taxable at peak provisional income, creating an elevated effective marginal rate and the potential for IRMAA Medicare surcharges roughly two years later.

Delaying to 70 with managed IRA withdrawals and Roth conversions in the meantime: lower income during the bridge years enables tax-efficient restructuring, and Social Security begins at a higher amount once income is more deliberately controlled. The after-tax lifetime income is materially higher under the delay strategy, despite the surface-level appearance of "leaving money on the table" by not collecting for three extra years.

Susan: Own Record vs. Divorced-Spouse Benefit

Own record at FRA: $900/month.

Divorced-spouse benefit at FRA: $1,200/month.

Potential divorced-survivor benefit, if her ex dies after having delayed his own claim: could approach $2,400–$3,000/month, depending on what he was actually receiving at the time.

Claiming only on her own record, without ever asking about the divorced-spouse option, would have cost Susan $300 a month she was legally entitled to. Over 20 years, that's $72,000 — not from a loophole or a clever strategy, but simply from understanding rules that already applied to her situation.

Taken together, these four profiles and their accompanying comparisons point to the same underlying lesson, repeated in slightly different forms: Social Security rewards people who ask the right questions before they file, not after. Jane asked how long she might live. Bob and Linda asked what would happen to the survivor. Carlos asked how his benefit would interact with his other income. Susan asked whether her own record was really her only option. None of these questions required a finance degree — they required only the willingness to pause, calculate, and ask, before making a decision that, in most cases, can't be undone.

The Bottom Line

Every mistake in this chapter shares the same root cause: a decision made without first asking the question that would have changed it. Jane's break-even calculation, Bob and Linda's survivor modeling, Carlos's provisional income check, and Susan's simple inquiry about her ex's record all took less than an hour combined — and each one was worth tens or hundreds of thousands of dollars over a lifetime. The rules in this book only pay off if you actually use them before you file, not after.

KEY TAKEAWAYS

• Run your own break-even calculation before claiming, even if you're fairly sure you already know what you'll decide. Jane's numbers turned a vague preference into a concrete, defensible plan.

• If you're married, model the survivor scenario explicitly — "what would my spouse receive if I died next year, under each claiming age we're considering?" — before either of you files. Twenty minutes of modeling can be worth hundreds of thousands of dollars.

• High earners with substantial other income should run a provisional income projection before claiming, not after. The tax consequences of timing can sometimes matter more than the raw benefit comparison.

• If you were married at least 10 years and are now divorced, ask Social Security directly whether you qualify for divorced-spouse or divorced-survivor benefits. Don't assume your own record is your only option.

• None of these four mistakes required complicated strategy to avoid — they required only the willingness to ask one specific question before filing, rather than discovering the answer years later when it was too late to change course.

Next up: how to turn everything in this book into an actual, living plan — the calculators and worksheets worth using, a simple annual review habit, and the most common questions readers ask once they're ready to actually file.

Chapter 12: Implement & Update Your Plan: Tools, FAQs, and Ongoing Checkups

Chapter at a Glance

What you'll learn in this chapter:

• Which calculators are actually worth your time — official SSA tools versus third-party options for couples and complex situations

• How to build a 45-minute annual review habit that keeps your plan current without becoming a chore

• Answers to the questions readers ask most often once they're actually ready to file

• A concrete action plan you can start this week, regardless of where you are in the process

Estimated reading time: 23 minutes

> ***FIELD NOTE*** *A finished retirement plan is a myth. I've never seen one that didn't need at least one adjustment within five years — a health change, a market swing, a new law, a spouse's decision shifting. The goal was never to get this perfectly right once. It's to build a habit of checking back in, so small corrections happen early, while they're still small.*

You've now worked through eleven chapters covering how Social Security benefits are calculated, when to claim them, how spousal and survivor rules function as a household system, how taxes interact with your benefits, what happens if you keep working, and the special cases that change the playbook for government workers, divorced individuals, and a handful of other situations. That's a genuinely comprehensive foundation. But understanding the rules and actually using them are two different things, and the gap between them is exactly where this final chapter lives.

This chapter is about implementation. We'll look at which calculators and worksheets are actually worth your time, how to build a simple annual review habit that keeps your plan current without turning into a chore, the questions readers ask most often once they're standing at the actual decision point, and finally, a concrete action plan you can start working through this week — regardless of whether you're 55 and just starting to think about this, or 66 and about to file.

Think of everything in the previous eleven chapters as the map. This chapter is about actually taking the first steps on the road, and knowing how to adjust course if the terrain looks different than expected once you're out there.

12.1 Calculators and Worksheets to Track Your Strategy

You don't need a finance degree to plan your Social Security claim well, but you do need accurate numbers — your numbers, not generic examples from a book. This section walks through which tools actually deliver that, and how to use them without getting lost in the process.

Start with the Official Tools

The most authoritative numbers available to you come directly from the Social Security Administration. Your "my Social Security" account at ssa.gov gives you a retirement calculator that pulls from your actual, current earnings record — not an estimate based on national averages, but your specific work history, with your specific dollar amounts. You can adjust your future earnings assumptions and see, in real time, how stopping work at 63 instead of 65 changes your projected benefit, or how the gap between claiming at 62 and 70 actually looks in your own numbers.

Beyond the basic estimator, the SSA offers a few additional tools worth knowing about. The Retirement Age Calculator shows your exact full retirement age and the precise monthly benefit adjustment for every possible claiming month — useful if you're trying to decide between, say, claiming in March versus claiming in September of the same year. The Earnings Test Calculator estimates how much of your benefit would be withheld if you work while claiming before your FRA, which directly extends the concepts from Chapter 7 into your own specific income numbers. And the Detailed Calculator, downloadable directly from ssa.gov, is the same underlying engine the SSA itself uses, letting you input a full year-by-year earnings projection if your income path is unusual or hard to estimate with a simple average.

These tools share one significant advantage over anything else available: they're built on the actual benefit formulas, not approximations or rules of thumb. When precision matters — and for a decision this size, it usually does — starting with the official SSA tools is always the right first move.

Third-Party Tools for Couples and Complex Situations

For married couples, the SSA's own tools can feel limited. They're built primarily around an individual's own record, and modeling spousal and survivor coordination — exactly the kind of analysis covered in Chapters 4 and 10 — often requires software designed specifically for that purpose. Several reputable financial websites and nonprofit organizations offer calculators built to handle these more complex scenarios.

When evaluating a third-party calculator, a few criteria separate the genuinely useful tools from the ones that will waste your time. Look for clear, visible assumptions — you want to know exactly what inflation rate, what cost-of-living adjustment, and what life expectancy the tool is using behind the scenes, not a black box that just spits out a single recommended age. Look for the ability to model multiple claiming sequences side by side, rather than a single linear recommendation; the whole point of the comparison thinking from Chapter 11 is seeing two or three paths next to each other, not being told there's only one right answer. And look for the ability to save or print your results, so you can bring them into a conversation with a spouse or a financial advisor instead of trying to describe a screen you saw once.

A genuinely good calculator should let you walk into a conversation with numbers in hand — not a fading memory of a chart you glanced at last week.

Your Personal Benefits Snapshot

In Chapter 3, you built a one-page benefits snapshot — your FRA, your work credits, your benefit estimates at 62, FRA, and 70, plus a brief tax note. If you haven't kept that document updated as you've worked through the rest of this book, now is the moment to do it. Pull your most recent estimates from the calculators above, and refresh that single page so it reflects everything you've learned since Chapter 3 — your coordinated couple strategy from Chapter 10, your tax awareness from Chapter 6, your special-case findings from Chapter 8 if any applied to you.

This document is what you hand a financial advisor instead of starting from scratch in every meeting. It's what you pull out the moment a major life event — a layoff, a diagnosis, a market downturn — prompts you to reconsider your plan. Keep it current, and every future decision becomes faster and more grounded in your actual numbers, rather than a vague memory of what you once calculated.

Flowcharts and Checklists as Living Documents

Chapter 9 gave you a decision tree and several scenario-specific checklists — for singles, couples, widows and widowers, and divorced claimants. These tools aren't meant to be used once and discarded. Print them and place them in a retirement planning binder, or save them in a dedicated folder on your computer or in cloud storage, somewhere you'll actually find them again without searching.

The goal is simple: when a question or a life change arises, you can pull up your existing framework rather than rebuilding your thinking from memory. Update these documents whenever rules change — the Social Security Fairness Act in 2025 is a clear recent example — or whenever your own situation shifts: a divorce, a new marriage, a new pension, a health diagnosis. Treat them the way you'd treat a will or a set of beneficiary designations: important enough to revisit periodically, not something you set once and forget for twenty years.

12.2 Annual Review: Adjusting Strategies as Circumstances Change

Your Social Security plan deserves the same periodic attention you already give your investment portfolio, your insurance coverage, and your estate documents. The good news is that this particular review doesn't require hours of work — roughly 45 minutes, once a year, covers it thoroughly.

Set a Date and Keep It

The single biggest reason annual reviews fail to happen is that they're never actually scheduled. Pick a specific, memorable anchor — tax time and your birthday month are two of the most common, simply because they're dates you're already thinking about your finances for other reasons — and put a standing appointment on your calendar. Treat it the same way you'd treat a dentist appointment: recurring, non-negotiable, and easy to reschedule slightly but never to skip entirely.

This isn't a multi-hour project, and it shouldn't feel like one. If your annual review is taking three hours, you're probably re-deriving information you should already have organized in your benefits snapshot and your checklists from earlier chapters. The review itself should be closer to a status check than a research project.

What to Review Each Year

Start by logging into your "my Social Security" account and pulling your current statement. Check your earnings record for any missing or incorrect years from the prior year specifically — this is the same earnings-record review from Chapter 1 and Chapter 3, just repeated annually so errors get caught while they're still easy to fix. Update your benefit estimates; they shift slightly almost every year as new earnings post to your record, and it's worth noting whether that shift changes your strategic thinking at all.

Next, scan for major legislative changes. Social Security rules can and do shift over time — the Social Security Fairness Act in 2025, which repealed WEP and GPO as covered in Chapter 8, is a significant recent example of exactly this kind of change. You don't need to track every policy proposal floated in Congress; you need to track the things that actually become law and might affect your specific situation. Subscribing to SSA email updates is probably the lowest-effort way to stay aware of genuine changes without drowning in political noise.

Finally, assess your own personal situation honestly. Did your health change in a way that affects your longevity expectations? Did you retire earlier or later than you'd originally planned? Did a marriage, divorce, or death in the family alter which benefit options are available to you? Did your savings grow or shrink in a way that changes whether you can comfortably afford to keep delaying? Update your plan in response to whatever you find — not dramatically, in most years, but deliberately.

When to Adjust Your Strategy

Your original claiming plan, whatever it was, is a starting point — not a contract you're locked into regardless of what happens next. Revisit it specifically whenever your health outlook changes materially, the way James's did in Chapter 5's case study. Revisit it when your work plans shift, earlier or later than you originally expected. Revisit it when a spouse or ex-spouse dies, since that event can open up survivor benefits you hadn't previously had access to. Revisit it when your savings take a significant hit, since that changes how much flexibility you genuinely have to delay claiming. And revisit it whenever major legislation changes the underlying rules, exactly as the 2025 Fairness Act did for anyone affected by WEP or GPO.

Most of these triggers don't require rebuilding your entire plan from scratch. They require adjusting one or two variables — your expected claiming age, your assumed longevity, your tax bracket — and rerunning the comparison using the same tools and frameworks you've already built throughout this book. That's the work of an afternoon, not a crisis. The crisis only happens when a major change goes unnoticed for years, because nobody was checking in on the plan at all.

12.3 FAQs and Resources for Continued Learning

Even after working through eleven chapters of detailed material, a handful of specific questions tend to come up again and again once people are actually standing at the decision point. This section collects the most common ones, along with where to turn for help that goes beyond what any book can offer.

Common Questions

What's the latest I can claim without losing out on any further increase?

Age 70. After that, delayed retirement credits stop accumulating entirely — there's no benefit at all to waiting past 70 to file, so there's no reason to delay any further once you reach that age.

Can I change my mind after I've already filed?

Within the first 12 months of filing, you can withdraw your application entirely, repay every benefit you've received (including anything paid to a spouse on your record), and refile later as though you'd never claimed at all. This option can only be used once in your lifetime. After you reach full retirement age, you can suspend your benefit instead — you won't need to repay anything you've already received, but your checks stop, delayed credits resume accumulating up to age 70, and any spousal benefits paid on your record are typically suspended at the same time.

What happens if I keep working after I've filed?

Before your full retirement age, the earnings test applies: earn above the annual limit and the SSA withholds $1 in benefits for every $2 you earn above it, exactly as covered in Chapter 7. Those withheld amounts generally come back as a permanent benefit increase once you reach FRA. After FRA, there's no earnings test at all — work as much as you want, with no reduction to your benefit. Continued strong earnings can even raise your benefit further, if they're high enough to replace a weaker year in your top 35.

How does divorce affect my benefits?

If your marriage lasted at least 10 consecutive years and you're now divorced, you may qualify for divorced-spouse benefits (up to 50% of your ex-spouse's PIA at your own FRA) and, if your ex has died, divorced-survivor benefits (up to 100% of what they were receiving). Your claim never reduces what your ex-spouse, or their current spouse, receives. Critically, the SSA won't proactively identify these options for you — as Susan's story in Chapter 11 showed clearly, you have to ask.

Were my benefit estimates ever affected by WEP or GPO?

If you have a pension from non-covered government work — certain teaching positions, police and fire roles, some state and local government jobs — and received a Social Security estimate before January 2025, it may well have reflected the old Windfall Elimination Provision or Government Pension Offset reductions covered in Chapter 8. Both were repealed by the Social Security Fairness Act for benefits payable January 2024 and later. If this applies to you, it's genuinely worth requesting an updated estimate rather than relying on anything you were told before the repeal.

When to Work with a Professional

The Social Security Administration itself is the right resource for a specific, narrow set of needs: confirming your exact benefit estimates, correcting errors in your earnings record, clarifying eligibility rules that apply to your situation, and actually processing your application when you're ready to file. What the SSA is not resourced or positioned to do is give you personalized financial planning advice — they can tell you what the rules say, but they won't tell you whether claiming at 67 or 70 is the right choice given your specific portfolio, your spouse's health, and your tax situation.

That broader, integrated advice is where a financial planner earns their value — specifically, a planner who treats Social Security as a core piece of retirement income planning, not an afterthought. When evaluating a potential advisor, ask directly how they model claiming decisions: do they run multi-year income projections that incorporate Social Security alongside your other assets, or do they treat it as a separate, simple decision made in isolation? Ask whether they coordinate Social Security timing with tax planning and portfolio withdrawal sequencing — exactly the kind of integration covered in Chapters 6 and 10. You want someone who sees the whole financial picture, with Social Security as one important piece inside it, not someone who only knows the Social Security piece in isolation from everything else.

Continuing to Learn

Social Security rules evolve. The 2025 Social Security Fairness Act is proof that even long-standing, deeply entrenched provisions like WEP and GPO can change, sometimes significantly, sometimes with real benefit to affected workers. Staying genuinely informed doesn't require constant vigilance — it requires the annual review habit from section 12.2, plus a willingness to ask, whenever something changes in the news or in your own life, "Does this affect my plan?"

The SSA's own publications, your annual statement, and reputable financial news sources are generally sufficient for staying current. Be cautious of advice that sounds confident but doesn't cite specific, current rules — as you've seen throughout this book, the details matter enormously, and outdated information (file-and-suspend strategies from before 2016, WEP and GPO assumptions from before 2025) can lead you toward a plan built on rules that no longer exist.

12.4 Your Action Plan for the Next Few Weeks

Knowledge without action doesn't move your retirement forward. To close out this book, here's a concrete, sequenced set of steps you can start working through this week, regardless of where you currently stand in the process.

Log into ssa.gov and pull your current statement. Download or print it so you have a fixed reference point, not just something you glanced at on a screen once.

Verify your earnings record line by line, exactly as covered in Chapters 1 and 3. Flag any year that looks wrong, and start gathering documentation — W-2s, tax returns, pay stubs — if you find a discrepancy.

Use the SSA's retirement calculator to estimate your benefits at 62, your full retirement age, and 70. Write the actual numbers down — not a rough memory of them, but the specific dollar figures.

If you're married, repeat the previous two steps for your spouse, and put both sets of numbers on a single page, exactly as described in Chapter 3.

Build or update your personal benefits snapshot worksheet, incorporating everything you've learned across this book — your coordinated strategy if you're a couple, your special-case findings if any chapter 8 provisions applied to you, and your tax notes from Chapter 6.

Run a basic break-even calculation between two specific claiming ages you're actually considering — not a generic comparison, but the two ages genuinely on the table for your situation.

Set a date for your first annual review and put it on your calendar right now, before you close this book. A date that doesn't exist on a calendar is a date that won't happen.

If your situation is complex — a public pension, a recent divorce, significant assets, multiple potential benefit types from different records — schedule a conversation with a financial planner who specializes in retirement income, and bring your benefits snapshot with you.

None of these steps requires more than an hour, and most take considerably less. Strung together, they move you from "I've read a book about Social Security" to "I have an actual plan, built on my actual numbers, that I know how to revisit when my life changes." That's the entire point of everything covered in the previous eleven chapters — not abstract mastery of the rules, but a concrete, usable plan sitting on your desk, ready whenever you need it.

The Bottom Line

Eleven chapters of rules and frameworks only matter if they turn into action. The tools in this chapter — the SSA's own calculators, your benefits snapshot, your decision tree and checklists from Chapter 9, a simple 45-minute annual review — are how you keep this plan alive instead of letting it sit, finished and forgotten, the moment you close this book. Social Security is, for most people, the single largest source of guaranteed, inflation-adjusted income they'll ever have. It deserves an actual plan, revisited regularly — not a one-time decision made on a whim at 62 and never reconsidered again.

KEY TAKEAWAYS

• Start with the SSA's own calculators for accuracy; turn to third-party tools when you need to model spousal and survivor coordination that the official tools don't handle as smoothly.

• Keep your one-page benefits snapshot from Chapter 3 updated as you learn more throughout this book — it's the document that makes every future decision, and every advisor conversation, faster and more grounded in your real numbers.

• Schedule a specific, recurring annual review — about 45 minutes, anchored to a date you'll actually remember. Use it to check your earnings record, update your estimates, and scan for legislative changes like the 2025 Fairness Act.

• Your original claiming plan is a starting point, not a contract. Revisit it when your health, work situation, marital status, savings, or the underlying law changes — most adjustments take an afternoon, not a crisis.

Close this book by actually doing something: pull your statement, verify your earnings, run your numbers, and put your first annual review on the calendar this week. A plan you've built but never act on is no better than no plan at all.

Conclusion

Here's what this book has really been about: taking a system designed by bureaucrats, for mass administration, and turning it into something you can actually use to make better decisions for your specific life.

Social Security is not one-size-fits-all, and if you've read this far, you already know why. Your claiming age, your spouse's claiming age, how you handle the years before benefits start, how you coordinate with your IRA and your pension — none of these are questions with a single universal answer printed somewhere in a government pamphlet. They're questions that require understanding the actual rules, and then applying honest judgment about your health, your savings, your tolerance for risk, and what you actually want your retirement to look like.

A few things are worth carrying with you specifically.

Your AIME and PIA determine what you've earned, full stop — that's the foundation everything else sits on. Your full retirement age sets the baseline. Every month you claim before it reduces your benefit permanently; every month after it, up to 70, increases it permanently. For most people in reasonable health, the math rewards patience. But patience requires the resources to actually wait, and not everyone has that, which is exactly why claiming early is sometimes the right call rather than a mistake to feel bad about.

If you're married, your Social Security decisions are shared decisions, whether you've been treating them that way or not. The higher earner's benefit is the household's single most important long-term asset — not because it's larger today, but because it becomes the survivor's income floor, potentially for decades after one of you is gone. Protect it accordingly, and have the conversation about what happens to whichever of you is left, before either of you files.

If you're divorced or widowed, your options are very likely larger than you currently think they are. The 10-year marriage rule opens divorced-spouse benefits that can meaningfully exceed your own record, and most people who qualify never find out. Survivor benefits offer a flexibility in sequencing that ordinary retirement benefits simply don't. Both are worth a direct conversation with Social Security before you assume your own record is the only option on the table.

On taxes: provisional income is the multiplier almost nobody sees coming. Every major income source in retirement — IRAs, pensions, capital gains, even municipal bond interest you assumed was invisible to the IRS — affects how much of your Social Security actually gets taxed. Managing that, particularly through Roth conversions and deliberate withdrawal sequencing, can make a real difference over a 20- or 30-year retirement.

On work: the earnings test scares people more than it should. It's a timing rule, not a permanent penalty — withheld benefits generally come back as a higher check once you reach full retirement age. The actual risk in claiming early while still working isn't the earnings test. It's locking in a permanently smaller benefit before you've genuinely run the numbers on what that costs you.

None of this requires you to become a Social Security expert. It requires you to do exactly what the case studies in Chapter 11 did: ask the one question that matters before you file, not after. Run your break-even. Model the survivor scenario. Check your provisional income. Ask whether you qualify for a benefit you didn't know existed. Each of those questions takes minutes. Skipping them can cost you years of income you were genuinely entitled to.

Social Security will likely keep changing in ways neither of us can fully predict — the 2025 repeal of WEP and GPO is proof that even deeply entrenched rules can shift. That's exactly why this book ends with an annual review habit rather than a single, final claiming age. Revisit your plan every year. Update it when your life changes. Treat it as a living decision, not a form you fill out once at 62 and never think about again.

Now take it from the page to the plan. Pull your statement. Run the break-even. Build the snapshot. Schedule the annual review. If you're married, do all of this together, not separately.

Social Security is, for most people, the single largest source of guaranteed, inflation-adjusted income they will ever have. It deserves more than a guess.

Before you go...

You've just finished this guide — and that puts you ahead of most people who'll reach retirement having never thought carefully about when and how to claim.

As a thank-you for reading, I've put together a free bonus tool exclusively for readers:

The Social Security Maximizer Checklist.

It covers the 10 decisions that determine how much you collect — not just on the day you claim, but for every month of the rest of your life.

Scan below or click the link to download it free.

It takes less than five minutes. Work through it once, and you'll know exactly which boxes are ticked — and which ones still need your attention before you file.

Scan for Your Free Social Security Maximizer Checklist

Free download — no credit card needed

Free Social Security Maximizer Checklist Download

Free Tools From Essential Retirement Guide

Five free calculators built to go alongside this series — no signup required to see your results.

Visit **essentialretirementguide.com** or scan any code below to open a tool on your phone or computer.

Social Security Claiming Age Calculator — When Should I File?
Compare your monthly benefit at age 62, your Full Retirement Age, and age 70 — and see which filing age gives you the most lifetime income based on your life expectancy.

https://www.essentialretirementguide.com/ss-calc

Social Security Tax Calculator — How Much of My Benefit Is Taxable?
Enter your income and filing status to see exactly how much of your Social Security benefit is subject to federal tax, based on the IRS provisional income formula.

https://www.essentialretirementguide.com/tax-calc

Roth Conversion Calculator — What's My Sweet Spot?
Find the maximum you can convert from a traditional IRA to a Roth this year without pushing income into a higher tax bracket. Uses the actual 2026 IRS federal tax brackets.

https://www.essentialretirementguide.com/roth-calc

RMD Calculator — What's My Required Minimum Distribution?
Find out exactly how much you're required to withdraw this year, when your deadline is, and what the penalty looks like if you miss it. Based on the IRS Uniform Lifetime Table for 2026.

https://www.essentialretirementguide.com/rmd

Early Withdrawal Penalty Calculator — What Would This Really Cost Me?
See the actual dollar cost of taking money out of a 401(k) or IRA before age 59½ — penalty and tax combined. Includes seven IRS penalty exceptions including the Rule of 55 and SEPP.

https://www.essentialretirementguide.com/penalty-calc

All tools are free to use. A personalized PDF report is available by email after you see your results.

Notes & Sources

Chapter 1: Understand the System: Social Security Basics Every Retiree Needs

Benefits Planner: Retirement | Delayed Retirement Credits | SSA. (n.d.). Www.ssa.gov. https://www.ssa.gov/benefits/retirement/planner/delayret.html

Greszler, R., & Greszler, R. (2025, August 7). *EPIC Explainer: How is your Social Security Benefit Calculated? - EPIC for America.* EPIC for America. https://epicforamerica.org/education-workforce-retirement/epic-explainer-how-is-your-social-security-benefit-calculated/

How Social Security Benefits are Calculated | Financial Freedom Wealth Management Group, LLC. (2025). Financialfreedomwmg.com. https://www.financialfreedomwmg.com/blog/how-social-security-benefits-are-calculated

OCACT. (2008, November 25). *Early or Late Retirement.* Www.ssa.gov. https://www.ssa.gov/OACT/quickcalc/early_late.html

Primary Insurance Amount. (n.d.). Www.ssa.gov. https://www.ssa.gov/oact/COLA/piaformula.html

Primary Insurance Amount: What it is, Calculations, and Examples. (n.d.). Investopedia. https://www.investopedia.com/terms/p/primary-insurance-amount.asp

Social Security Retirement Benefit Calculation. (n.d.). Www.ssa.gov. https://www.ssa.gov/OACT/ProgData/retirebenefit2.html

Social Security Administration. (n.d.). *Social Security Benefit Amounts.* Www.ssa.gov. https://www.ssa.gov/oact/cola/Benefits.html

Social Security: Benefit Calculation. (2026). Congress.gov. https://www.congress.gov/crs-product/R46658

The Social Security Benefit Formula | Bipartisan Policy Center. (n.d.). Bipartisanpolicy.org. https://bipartisanpolicy.org/explainer/social-security-benefit-formula/

Chapter 2: Your Claiming Timeline: When to File for Maximum Impact

A Guide on Taking Social Security. (n.d.). Schwab Brokerage. https://www.schwab.com/learn/story/guide-on-taking-social-security

Benefits Planner: Retirement | Filing Rules for Retirement and Spouses Benefits | SSA. (n.d.). Www.ssa.gov. https://www.ssa.gov/benefits/retirement/planner/claiming.html

Block, S. (2024, March 22). *Eight Strategies for Deciding When to File For Social Security*. Kiplinger. https://www.kiplinger.com/retirement/social-security/strategies-for-deciding-when-to-file-for-social-security

Break Even Calculator for Social Security. (2026). Carrolladvisory.com. https://www.carrolladvisory.com/free-break-even-calculator-for-social-security

Holmes, T. E. (2025, December 11). *What is the Social Security break-even age?* AARP. https://www.aarp.org/social-security/faq/break-even-age/

Patience is sometimes a virtue when it comes to claiming Social Security | TIAA. (2022). Tiaa.org. https://www.tiaa.org/public/invest/services/wealth-management/perspectives/social-security-claiming-strategies

Plan for Retirement. (2025). Social Security. https://www.ssa.gov/retirement/plan-for-retirement

Social Security benefits help maximize your clients' outcomes. (2026). Vanguard.com. https://advisors.vanguard.com/insights/article/social-security-benefits-help-maximize-your-clients-outcomes

Social Security | Readjust your claiming strategy | Fidelity. (2025, June 16). Fidelity.com. https://www.fidelity.com/learning-center/personal-finance/retirement/readjust-your-claiming-strategy

Wondering When to Claim Social Security? 5 Factors to Consider. (2025). RegionsBank. https://www.regions.com/insights/wealth/article/when-to-claim-social-security

Chapter 3: Know Your Numbers: Build a Simple Personal Benefits Snapshot

Diak, J. J. (2025, March 3). *Why Reviewing Your Social Security Statement Matters and How to Get Started.* Oatley-Diak. https://www.oatleydiak.com/post/how-to-review-social-security-statement

How can I get a Social Security Statement? (2023, December 8). Social Security. https://www.ssa.gov/faqs/en/questions/KA-01741.html

Purple. (2024, December 12). *Understanding Your Social Security Statement.* Withpurple.com; Purple. https://www.withpurple.com/post/understanding-your-social-security-statement

Reading. (2019, March 6). *The Dala Group.* The Dala Group. https://thedalagroup.com/blog/what-to-look-for-on-your-social-security-benefit-statement

Social Security Administration. (n.d.). *Social Security Benefit Amounts.* Www.ssa.gov. https://www.ssa.gov/oact/cola/Benefits.html

Social Security Administration. (2025). *Contribution and Benefit Base*. Ssa.gov. https://www.ssa.gov/OACT/COLA/cbb.html

What is the current maximum amount of taxable earnings for Social Security? (2025, January 2). Ssa.gov. https://www.ssa.gov/faqs/en/questions/KA-02387.html

What is a Social Security statement? | Fidelity. (2025, September 29). Fidelity.com. https://www.fidelity.com/learning-center/personal-finance/social-security-statement

Your Social Security Statement: A Personalized Guide to Your Benefits. (2026, January 8). Hartford Funds. https://www.hartfordfunds.com/insights/investor-insight/navigating-longevity/social-security/your-social-security-statement-a-personalized-guide-to-your-benefits.html

the, U. (2024, September 19). *Understanding the Redesigned Social Security Statement: A Guide to Maximizing Your Benefits - Best Tax Accountant in Woodbridge, VA | JS Morlu LLC*. Best Tax Accountant in Woodbridge, va | JS Morlu LLC. https://www.jsmorlu.com/retirement-planning/social-security-statement/

Chapter 4: Spousal & Survivor Strategies: Protecting Household Income

Benefits Planner: Retirement | Filing Rules for Retirement and Spouses Benefits | SSA. (n.d.). Www.ssa.gov. https://www.ssa.gov/benefits/retirement/planner/claiming.html

Backman, M. (2026, March 5). *Spousal Social Security Benefits: 3 Things All Retired Couples Should Know*. The Motley Fool. https://www.fool.com/retirement/2026/03/05/spousal-social-security-benefits-3-things-all-reti/

Markowitz, A. (2022, September 21). *Social Security Claiming Strategies for Couples*. AARP. https://www.aarp.org/social-security/claiming-strategies-for-couples/

OACT. (n.d.). *Benefits for Spouses*. Www.ssa.gov. https://www.ssa.gov/oact/quickcalc/spouse.html

Spousal Benefits: An Often Overlooked Key to Maximizing Social Security Benefits for Couples. (2023, August 24). Hartford Funds. https://www.hartfordfunds.com/practice-management/client-conversations/financial-planning/an-often-overlooked-key-to-maximizing-social-security-benefits-for-couples.html

Social Security tips for couples | Fidelity. (2025, December 12). Fidelity.com. https://www.fidelity.com/viewpoints/retirement/social-security-tips-for-couples

Social Security tips for married couples | Vanguard. (n.d.). Investor.vanguard.com. https://investor.vanguard.com/investor-resources-education/social-security/strategies-for-married-couples

Thrivent. (2025, January 10). *Social Security For Married Couples: Maximize Your Benefits | Thrivent*. Thrivent.com. https://

www.thrivent.com/insights/social-security/maximizing-social-security-for-married-couples-how-it-works-spousal-strategies-to-consider

T. Rowe Price Personal Investor - How surviving spouses can optimize their Social Security claiming strategies. (2025). Troweprice.com. https://www.troweprice.com/personal-investing/resources/insights/how-surviving-spouses-can-optimize-their-social-security-claiming-strategies.html

Young, R., Reichenstein, W., & Meyer, W. (2025, September 26). *How can I create a smarter strategy for claiming my Social Security benefits?* T. Rowe Price; T.Row.Price. https://www.troweprice.com/personal-investing/resources/insights/how-can-i-create-a-smarter-strategy-for-claiming-my-social-security-benefits.html

Chapter 5: Maximize Lifetime Payouts: Practical Strategies that Work

6 ways to help maximize Social Security | Fidelity. (2026, February 13). Fidelity.com. https://www.fidelity.com/learning-center/personal-finance/maximize-social-security

Benefits Planner: Retirement | Delayed Retirement Credits | SSA. (n.d.). Www.ssa.gov. https://www.ssa.gov/benefits/retirement/planner/delayret.html

Earn, Baby, Earn: The Key to Maximizing Your Social Security. (2024, September 18). Hartford Funds. https://www.hartfordfunds.com/practice-management/client-conversations/financial-planning/earn-baby-earn-the-key-to-maximizing-your-social-security.html

Practical Retirement Guidance: How To Make the Most of Your Social Security Benefits. (2026). Smith Anglin. https://smithanglin.com/blogs/insights/practical-retirement-guidance-how-to-make-the-most-of-your-social-security-benefits

Patience is sometimes a virtue when it comes to claiming Social Security | TIAA. (2022). Tiaa.org. https://www.tiaa.org/public/invest/services/wealth-management/perspectives/social-security-claiming-strategies

Retirement Researcher. (2015, November 5). Retirement Researcher. https://retirementresearcher.com/philosophy-of-social-security-claiming-strategies/

SSA, O. (n.d.). *What are delayed retirement credits and how do they increase my old-age benefit amount?* Www.ssa.gov. https://www.ssa.gov/OP_Home/cfr20/404/404-0313.htm

Social Security: One decision, a lifetime of benefits. (2025, October 22). Transamerica. https://www.transamerica.com/knowledge-place/social-security-one-decision-lifetime-benefits

Siskos, C., & LeValley, D. (2021, May 6). *These Claiming Strategies Could Add Thousands to Your Social Security Checks*. Kiplinger. https://www.kiplinger.com/retirement/social-security/602749/whats-your-strategy-for-maximizing-social-security-benefits

Western. (2023, October 9). *What Are Delayed Retirement Credits?* Westernsouthern.com; Western & Southern Financial Group. https://www.westernsouthern.com/retirement/what-are-delayed-retirement-credits

Chapter 6: Taxes and Social Security: Keep More of What You Earn

Charles Schwab. (n.d.). Www.schwab.com. https://www.schwab.com/learn/story/social-security-is-taxable-how-to-minimize-taxes

Exempt Amounts Under the Earnings Test. (2020). Ssa.gov. https://www.ssa.gov/OACT/COLA/rtea.html

IRS reminds taxpayers their Social Security benefits may be taxable | Internal Revenue Service. (n.d.). Www.irs.gov. https://www.irs.gov/newsroom/irs-reminds-taxpayers-their-social-security-benefits-may-be-taxable

Long Range Solvency Provisions. (2025). Ssa.gov. https://www.ssa.gov/oact/solvency/provisions/taxbenefit.html

Reducing taxes on Social Security. (2025, July 30). Fidelity.com. https://www.fidelity.com/learning-center/personal-finance/retirement/reducing-taxes-on-social-security

Research: Income Taxes on Social Security Benefits. (n.d.). Social Security Administration Research, Statistics, and Policy Analysis. https://www.ssa.gov/policy/docs/issuepapers/ip2015-02.html

Social Security Benefit Taxation Highlights. (2025). Congress.gov. https://www.congress.gov/crs-product/IF11397

Tips for seniors in preparing their taxes | Internal Revenue Service. (2016). Irs.gov. https://www.irs.gov/individuals/seniors-retirees/tips-for-seniors-in-preparing-their-taxes

Taxes in Retirement: How to Reduce Taxes on Your Withdrawals. (n.d.). Merrill Lynch. https://www.ml.com/articles/taxes-in-retirement.html

Young, R. (2025, April 2). *What to know about Social Security benefits and your taxes.* T. Rowe Price; T.Row.Price. https://www.troweprice.com/en/us/insights/the-impact-of-social-security-benefits-on-your-taxes

Chapter 7: Work, Part-Time Income, and Benefits: What Continuing to Earn Means

Benefits Planner: Retirement | Receiving Benefits While Working | SSA. (n.d.). Www.ssa.gov. https://www.ssa.gov/benefits/retirement/planner/whileworking.html

Can you work and collect Social Security benefits? | Vanguard. (2025). Vanguard.com. https://investor.vanguard.com/investor-resources-education/social-security/collecting-benefits-while-working

Evaluating the Initial Impact of Eliminating the Retirement Earnings Test. (2004, May). Social Security Administration Research, Statistics, and Policy Analysis. https://www.ssa.gov/policy/docs/ssb/v65n1/v65n1p1.html

How working after you retire can affect your Social Security benefits. (2026). Protective.com . https://www.protective.com/learn/how-working-after-you-retire-can-affect-your-social-security-benefits

Huffman, L. (2026, February 27). *The 1 Social Security Change You Probably Missed This Year.* Aol.com; AOL. https://www.aol.com/articles/1-social-security-change-probably-110700178.html

Kotlikoff, L. (2021, February 4). *Ask Larry: Will Working Part Time Lower My Social Security Retirement Benefits?* Forbes. https://www.forbes.com/sites/kotlikoff/2021/02/04/ask-larry-will-part-time-work-lower-my-social-security-retirement-benefits/

LeValley, D. (2025, October 29). *The Social Security Earnings Test: Know This Rule Before Working in Retirement.* Kiplinger. https://www.kiplinger.com/retirement/social-security/social-security-earnings-test-explainer

Program Explainer: Retirement Earnings Test. (2015). Ssa.gov. https://www.ssa.gov/policy/docs/program-explainers/retirement-earnings-test.html

Retirement Earnings Test Calculator. (n.d.). Www.ssa.gov. https://www.ssa.gov/oact/cola/RTeffect.html

What happens if I work and get Social Security retirement benefits? (2025, January 2). Ssa.gov. https://www.ssa.gov/faqs/en/questions/KA-01921.html

Chapter 8: Special Cases & Exceptions: Rules That Change the Playbook

National Education Association. (2025). *FAQs About the Windfall Elimination Provision | NEA*. Nea.org. https://www.nea.org/professional-excellence/student-engagement/tools-tips/faqs-about-windfall-elimination-provision

Program Explainer: Windfall Elimination Provision. (n.d.). Www.ssa.gov. https://www.ssa.gov/policy/docs/program-explainers/windfall-elimination-provision.html

Q&A: How will the Social Security Fairness Act impact me? - IAFF. (2025, January 5). IAFF. https://www.iaff.org/news/qa-how-will-the-social-security-fairness-act-impact-me/

Research: Social Security Beneficiaries Affected by the Windfall Elimination Provision in 2006. (2008, October). Social Security Administration Research, Statistics, and Policy Analysis. https://www.ssa.gov/policy/docs/ssb/v68n2/v68n2p21.html

Social Security Fairness Act FAQ's | U.S. Representative Brittany Pettersen. (2024). House.gov. https://pettersen.house.gov/services/social-security-fairness-act-faq-s.htm

Social Security Fairness Act: Windfall Elimination Provision (WEP) and Government Pension Offset (GPO) update | SSA. (2025). Ssa.gov. https://www.ssa.gov/benefits/retirement/social-security-fairness-act.html

Social Security & Your CalPERS Pension | CalPERS. (2025, February 13). Ca.gov. https://www.calpers.ca.gov/members/retirement-benefits/service-disability-retirement/social-security-and-your-pension

TurboTaxBlogTeam. (2025, March 7). *Social Security Fairness Act: Benefits, Impact, & More | Intuit TurboTax Blog*. Blog. https://blog.turbotax.intuit.com/breaking-news/social-security-fairness-act-109805/

What the Repeal of the Windfall Elimination Provision (WEP) Means for Social Security Benefits. (2025). Corebridgefinancial.com. https://www.corebridgefinancial.com/rs/home/financial-education/education-center/retirement-planning/what-the-repeal-of-the-windfall-elimination-provision-means

Windfall Elimination Provision - U.S. Embassy & Consulates in Japan. (2025, April 16). U.S. Embassy & Consulates in Japan. https://jp.usembassy.gov/services/social-security/wep/

Chapter 9: Simple Decision Frameworks: Flowcharts and Checklists to Claim Confidently

A Comparison of Free Online Tools for Individuals Deciding When to Claim Social Security Benefits. (2016, December). Social Security Administration Research, Statistics, and Policy Analysis. https://www.ssa.gov/policy/docs/rsnotes/rsn2016-03.html

Duderstadt, C. (2024, April 18). *Modern Wealth Management*. Modern Wealth Management. https://www.modwm.com/financial-checklist-after-the-death-of-a-spouse/

FREE GUIDE: When, Why, and How Should I File for Social Security? (2018). Financeinsights.net. https://financeinsights.net/gmxgh1WYghrkJxP

Hutchinson, D. (2024, December 20). *When to Take Social Security | Break-Even Age Chart and Examples*. Letsassemble.com; Assembly. https://www.letsassemble.com/blog/when-to-take-social-security

Kitces, M. (2018, July 16). *Michael Kitces*. Nerd's Eye View | Kitces.com. https://www.kitces.com/blog/fppathfinder-financial-planning-checklists-and-flowcharts-due-diligence/

Markowitz, A. (2025, April 28). *Social Security Survivor Benefits: 10 Things Spouses Need to Know*. AARP. https://www.aarp.org/social-security/survivor-benefits-eligibility-checklist/

Page Restricted. (2026). Fppathfinder.com. https://www.fppathfinder.com/six-more-ways-checklists-and-flowcharts-will-help-you/

Survivor benefits | SSA. (2024, June 11). Www.ssa.gov. https://www.ssa.gov/survivor

Social Security and Medicare Hub. (2025). Jpmorgan.com. https://am.jpmorgan.com/us/en/asset-management/adv/insights/retirement-insights/social-security-medicare-hub/

The Benefit Receipt Patterns and Labor Market Experiences of Older Workers Who Were Denied Social Security Disability Insurance Benefits on the Basis of Work Capacity. (2020, May). Social Security Administration Research, Statistics, and Policy Analysis. https://www.ssa.gov/policy/docs/ssb/v80n2/v80n2p25.html

Chapter 10: Advanced Coordination: Couples' Strategies for Peak Lifetime Income

ARQWealth. (2025, October 25). *ARQ Wealth Advisors.* ARQ Wealth Advisors. https://arqwealth.com/social-security-strategies-for-married-couples-to-maximize-benefits/

Gigante, S. (2025, April 10). *Social Security strategies for spouses | MassMutual.* Massmutual.com. https://blog.massmutual.com/retiring-investing/what-married-people-should-consider-when-filing-for-social-security

Markowitz, A. (2022, September 21). *Social Security Claiming Strategies for Couples*. AARP. https://www.aarp.org/social-security/claiming-strategies-for-couples/

Married? Know your Social Security benefits and options. (2026). Athene.com. https://www.athene.com/smart-strategies/married-know-your-social-security-benefits-and-options.html

Spousal Benefits: An Often Overlooked Key to Maximizing Social Security Benefits for Couples. (2023, August 24). Hartford Funds. https://www.hartfordfunds.com/practice-management/client-conversations/financial-planning/an-often-overlooked-key-to-maximizing-social-security-benefits-for-couples.html

Social Security tips for married couples | Vanguard. (n.d.). Investor.vanguard.com. https://investor.vanguard.com/investor-resources-education/social-security/strategies-for-married-couples

Strategies for Married Couples - Mary Beth Franklin | Retire Pro. (2022, December 28). Mary Beth Franklin | Retire Pro. https://marybethfranklin.com/strategies-for-married-couples/

Smart Social Security Strategies for Married Couples: A Comprehensive Guide. (2025). Key.com. https://www.key.com/wealth/our-insights/articles/smart-social-security-strategies-married-couples.html

Thrivent. (2025, January 10). *Social Security For Married Couples: Maximize Your Benefits | Thrivent*. Thrivent.com. https://

www.thrivent.com/insights/social-security/maximizing-social-security-for-married-couples-how-it-works-spousal-strategies-to-consider

for, S. (2025, December 15). *Cornerstone Wealth Group*. Cornerstone Wealth Group. https://www.cwgadvisors.com/blog/coordinating-social-security-strategies-for-highnetworth-married-couples

Chapter 11: Real-World Case Studies: Learn from Practical Examples

Incentivizing Delayed Claiming of Social Security Retirement Benefits Before Reaching the Full Retirement Age. (2014, November). Social Security Administration Research, Statistics, and Policy Analysis. https://www.ssa.gov/policy/docs/ssb/v74n4/v74n4p21.html

Knoll, M. (2011). *Behavioral and Psychological Aspects of the Retirement Decision*. Social Security Administration Research, Statistics, and Policy Analysis. https://www.ssa.gov/policy/docs/ssb/v71n4/v71n4p15.html

Marcotte, Z., & Marcotte, Z. (2025, July). *Social Security Mistakes High Earners Often Make (and How to Avoid Them) | Berkshire Money Management*. Berkshire Money Management. https://berkshiremm.com/social-security-mistakes-high-earners-often-make-and-how-to-avoid-them/

Social Security Benefits: Strategies for Divorcing Spouses. (2018, December 26). Miles Mason Family Law Group, PLC. https://memphisdivorce.com/social-security-benefits-strategies-for-divorcing-spouses/

Shedden, M. (2025, July 25). *How Divorced Retirees Can Maximize Their Social Security Benefits: A Case Study*. Kiplinger. https://www.kiplinger.com/retirement/social-security/how-divorced-retirees-can-maximize-their-social-security-benefits

Social Security: For some, early claiming is better. (2025). Vanguard.com. https://corporate.vanguard.com/content/corporatesite/us/en/corp/articles/social-security-for-some-claiming-early-better.html

Social Security Case Studies: What's at Stake for Single, Married, Divorced and Widowed Retirees? - Wolters Kluwer. (2024). Cchcpelink.com. https://www.cchcpelink.com/case

Which Social Security Claiming Strategy Generates the Highest Legacy Value? (2023). Financial Planning Association. https://www.financialplanningassociation.org/learning/publications/journal/JAN23-which-social-security-claiming-strategy-generates-highest-legacy-value-OPEN

Whitaker, M. (2025, August 19). *How to Retire at 60: A Complete Case Study for Early Retirement Planning*. Early Retirement Advice. https://earlyretirementadvice.com/2025/08/19/967/

jillian. (2025, August 7). *Planning Your Social Security Strategy: What to Consider When Claiming Benefits | Coldstream.* Coldstream.com. https://www.coldstream.com/insights/planning-your-social-security-strategy-what-to-consider-when-claiming-benefits/

Chapter 12: Implement & Update Your Plan: Tools, FAQs, and Ongoing Checkups

Benefits Planner: Retirement | Retirement Age Calculator | SSA. (n.d.). Www.ssa.gov. https://www.ssa.gov/benefits/retirement/planner/ageincrease.html

Benefit Calculators - Estimate Your Benefit. (n.d.). Www.ssa.gov. https://www.ssa.gov/OACT/anypia/index.html

Benefit Calculators | SSA. (n.d.). Www.ssa.gov. https://www.ssa.gov/benefits/calculators/

Benefits Planner: Retirement | Online Benefits Calculator | SSA. (n.d.). Www.ssa.gov. https://www.ssa.gov/benefits/retirement/planner/AnypiaApplet.html

Levine, J. (2021, February 17). *Michael Kitces.* Nerd's Eye View | Kitces.com. https://www.kitces.com/blog/my-social-security-statement-projected-benefits-correction-earnings-history/

Open Social Security: Free, Open-Source Social Security Calculator. (n.d.). Opensocialsecurity.com. https://opensocialsecurity.com/

OACT. (2014, May 27). *Social Security Quick Calculator*. Www.ssa.gov. https://www.ssa.gov/OACT/quickcalc/

Retirement planning tools | USAGov. (n.d.). Www.usa.gov. https://www.usa.gov/retirement-planning-tools

Social Security Calculator | Benefits Estimator. (n.d.). Bankrate. https://www.bankrate.com/retirement/social-security-benefits-calculator/

Waggoner, J. (2024, November 21). *Social Security Calculator*. AARP. https://www.aarp.org/social-security/benefits-calculator/

Next in The Essential Retirement Strategy Series

THE ESSENTIAL RETIREMENT TAX PLANNING GUIDE

How to Keep More of Your Retirement Income and Avoid Costly Tax Mistakes

Taxes don't disappear in retirement—and without proper planning, they can significantly reduce the income you've worked hard to build.

The Essential Retirement Tax Planning Guide explains how different sources of retirement income are taxed and how thoughtful withdrawal strategies can help preserve more of your savings over time.

Inside this upcoming guide, you'll learn how to:

• Understand how 401(k)s, IRAs, Roth accounts, and pensions are taxed
• Avoid unexpected tax bills from required minimum distributions (RMDs)
• Coordinate withdrawals across accounts to improve tax efficiency
• Recognize how income levels can affect the taxation of Social Security benefits

This practical guide will help you make more informed decisions, reduce unnecessary tax burdens, and create a more efficient retirement income strategy.

www.ingramcontent.com/pod-product-compliance
Lightning Source LLC
LaVergne TN
LVHW010718061126
851857LV00014B/1237
9791399270426